a guide to
acting
on AIDS:

Understanding the Global AIDS Pandemic and Responding Through Faith and Action

Edited by:

Jyl Hall,

Laura Barton, Michaela Dodd, James Pedrick, Jackie Yoshimura

Published in partnership with World Vision Resources

Authentic Publishing
We welcome your questions and comments.

USA   PO Box 444, 285 Lynnwood Ave, Tyrone, GA, 30290
      www.authenticbooks.com

UK   9 Holdom Avenue, Bletchley, Milton Keynes, Bucks, MK1 1QR, UK
      www.authenticmedia.co.uk

India   Logos Bhavan, Medchal Road, Jeedimetla Village,
        Secunderabad 500 055, A.P.

A Guide To Acting On Aids
ISBN-13: 978-1-932805-80-2
ISBN-10: 1-932805-80-X

Published in partnership with World Vision.
34834 Weyerhaeuser Way South, P.O. Box 9716, Federal Way, WA 98063 USA
www.worldvision.org

Cover design: Creative**Solutions**, World Vision
Interior design: Creative**Solutions**, World Vision and Paul Lewis

Printed in the United States of America

Contents

5-79

115992

Acknowledgments

General Editor:
Jyl Hall

Contributing Editors:
Laura Barton
Michaela Dodd
James Pedrick
Jackie Yoshimura

Contributing Writers:
Jyl Hall
Bard Luippold
Nathalie Moberg
James Pedrick

Special Thanks:
Chevonne Carnahan
Kelley Charlston
Michaela Dodd
Heather Ferriera
John Gomes
Betsey Grabinski
Selena Koosmann
John Leckie
B.J. Louws
Milana McLead
Rebecca Oehler
Mircea Poeana
Joel Shoemaker
Ryan Smith

Two thousand years after Jesus gave the church the parable of the Good Samaritan, we are still asking the question, "Who is my neighbor?" And we're still getting the answer wrong. Today, the parable compels us to challenge our own community of faith, an American church that is belatedly responding to the AIDS pandemic, which last year alone killed 3 million people.

The parable addresses one of the most profound questions in all of Scripture: "Who is my neighbor?" We find Jesus' answer in the actions of the four main characters: the victim, the priest, the Levite, and the Samaritan.

The only thing we know for certain about the victim is that he was in dire need: beaten, wounded, bleeding, and possibly dying. We don't know why he was beaten. He may have been an "innocent" victim, unjustly attacked, or a robber, beaten by fellow thieves. Jesus did not indicate whether the man beaten was at fault.

Today, as many as 46 million people are infected with the AIDS virus. If Jesus, in the parable of the Good Samaritan, did not distinguish whether he was a victim because of sinful behavior or an innocent victim, should we? We are bound by Scripture to respond to all those beaten and left by this devastating virus.

Scripture makes clear who has the right to judge: God, not us. Yet we judge people with AIDS. We conveniently forget that we too would be dead if we faced such a certain death for any of our sins—including indifference to those who are suffering.

The sin of indifference is, of course, the only one Jesus condemns in the story, and it is embodied by the next two characters: the priest and the Levite who represent the religious establishment of the day. We are told that they saw the man and yet they passed by on the other side of the road, knowing what was right but failing to act.

In 2002, World Vision commissioned a study through the Barna Research Group to determine the willingness of the Christian community to get involved in fighting the AIDS epidemic. When evangelical Christians were asked whether they would be willing to donate money to help children orphaned by AIDS, only 3% answered that they definitely would. More than half said that they probably or definitely would not help.

How should the Christian community respond to those affected by AIDS? James 4:17 states, "Anyone, then, who knows the good he ought to do and doesn't do it, sins" (NIV). In light of this, how should the Christian community respond to the victims of HIV/AIDS? The fourth character of Jesus' parable shows us.

Despite the fact that Samaritans were often despised by the Jews, this Samaritan saw the man at the side of the road "and took pity on him."

How can the American church, with all its resources and influence, fail to respond proportionally to the greatest problem facing the world? I am certain that God expects His people to act, not remain silent. Those suffering the brunt of this pandemic are millions of widows and orphans who have done nothing wrong. I am certain that God sees these widows and orphans as our neighbors, lying beaten and bleeding on the side of the road, helpless and needing our help. And I am certain that He calls us to stop, show compassion, comfort them, bind up their wounds, and see that they and their children are cared for.

How? By advocating for right theology in our churches and right policies by our government. By praying for people who are living with AIDS, for the children they leave behind, and for their caregivers. By volunteering with local organizations and by supporting our brothers and sisters in Africa and elsewhere in their efforts to stop this epidemic and care for those whose lives have already been shattered.

This book will provide an overview of the AIDS pandemic and many of the key problems surrounding this immense issue. I urge you to read this book and take what is says to heart. But please, do not stop there. It will take persistent action on the part of the Church, and young people especially, to make a significant difference in this world.

Jesus ends the Parable of the Good Samaritan with a powerful challenge. When Jesus asks which of the three men had been a neighbor to the man who fell into the hands of robbers, the response given is "The one who had mercy on him."

Jesus then concludes with what is perhaps the most powerful moral teaching in all of history, a command of just four words: "Go and do likewise."

— Richard E. Stearns
President of World Vision in the United States

"Learn to do good; seek justice, correct oppression; bring justice to the fatherless, plead the widow's cause. 'Come now, let us reason together, says the LORD: though your sins are like scarlet, they shall be as white as snow; though they are red like crimson, they shall become like wool.'" (Isaiah 1:17–18, NLT)

do you see orange?

It was a typical day in February. Gray skies stretched across Seattle. Rain threatened. It wasn't a hopeful sight.

But hope was alive on the small, Christian liberal arts campus of Seattle Pacific University. Color blossomed in the most unlikely of places as young college students answered their generation's call to seek justice and bring hope. One out of every 20 students wore a bright orange T-shirt that was labeled "ORPHAN" to represent the proportion of children orphaned by AIDS in sub-Saharan Africa.

Students participate in the "Do You See Orange?" T-shirt campaign at Seattle Pacific University. 1 in 20 students wear in an "ORPHAN" shirt to represent the statistic that presently 1 in 20 children in Africa are orphaned by HIV/AIDS.

For many students, the sudden appearance of orange was a surprise. Until that day, many had been ignorant of the impact AIDS is having around the world, particularly on children.

Throughout the week, students noticed bright orange signs around campus that asked one simple question: "Do You See Orange?" Suddenly, their campus was infected. Friends and peers in classrooms and dorms were walking around wearing "ORPHAN" T-shirts. "Do You See Orange?" posters were replaced with "Do You See Orphans?" posters. The campus was inundated with statistics:

- 1 in 20 children in Africa are orphaned by AIDS.[1]

- Every 14 seconds another child is orphaned by AIDS.[2]

- Nearly 8,000 people will die today because of AIDS.[3]

- In some countries, more than 40% of the population are infected with HIV.[4]

- Life expectancy in sub-Saharan Africa has plummeted. For example, AIDS has reduced Zimbabwe's life expectancies from 70 years to 39 years.[5]

The most powerful statement was from those students who were wearing orange T-shirts. They were representing those who, if they were living in sub-Saharan Africa, would be orphaned.

a movement began

How did this movement start on a small, Christian liberal arts campus? It began with three college students determined to make a difference.

James Pedrick and Lisa Krohn, interns at World Vision the summer of 2004, were sitting in a meeting—one of a series designed to orient and educate interns working at World Vision's U.S. headquarters in Federal Way. Steve Haas, World Vision's vice president for church relations, stood before the interns passionately sharing the reality of how AIDS is destroying millions who already struggle in desperately poor countries.

"He was very candid about the church's lack of response to AIDS, and the need for our generation to act," recalled James, who went into that meeting, never expecting that he would leave with his life's direction forever altered. "Coming out of that meeting Lisa and I knew we were called to do something at Seattle Pacific."

Soon, their friend Jackie Yoshimura was involved as well. Jackie also felt that she would choose each day to respond to this pandemic as a response to Christ and His blessing in her life. As summer ended and their senior year began, these three students were determined to raise awareness on their campus and motivate their fellow students to change the world. Three students formed Acting on AIDS, an initiative to create awareness and promote activism on their campus.

Student designed banners and posters are prominently displayed around campus promoting the T-shirt campaign.

The idea behind the "Do You See Orange?" campaign was to breathe life into impersonal statistics so that fellow students could feel their impact and contemplate their significance. The Acting on AIDS student leadership was motivated by the fact that 1 in 20 children in sub-Saharan Africa have been orphaned by AIDS and that this number would double in 10 years. Through the orange T-shirts, they found a way to make that statistic understood by everyone else on their campus.

During the T-shirt campaign, hundreds of students learned more about the global AIDS pandemic through fellow students and guest speakers. As a result, many pursued volunteer and intern opportunities with various organizations, participated in community service with local organizations, raised resources for communities most affected by AIDS, and engaged in political advocacy.

small steps of faith

Students continued to promote the movement at Seattle Pacific through various activities designed to educate and increase awareness. Meanwhile, students at other Christian colleges learned about the movement and wanted to start similar activities on their own campuses.

Eventually the program of Acting on AIDS spread to other campuses and formed a national network of Christian college students who are committed to change the face of AIDS. With full institutional support from World Vision, in one year the Acting on AIDS movement grew from one campus to more than 40 Christian college chapters that are changing hearts on their campuses, creating awareness in their communities, and advocating for those impacted by the global AIDS pandemic.

With a few small steps of faith, ordinary students created a grass-roots movement that changed the course of their campuses and moved their peers and institutions toward caring about the millions infected, widowed, and orphaned by HIV and AIDS.

How it Works

The Acting on AIDS structure exists on 2 levels—as individual chapters on college campuses and as the collective national network of student leaders involved in the program.

At the local level, each Acting on AIDS campus chapter is formed by a group of student leaders at individual campuses. Chapters exist to engage their students, faculty, and administration on the global AIDS pandemic and to reach out to their local communities and churches to increase awareness and activism of the crisis. Chapters typically consist of a team of core leaders who create and organize efforts as well as a larger membership of students who actively participate in Acting on AIDS campaigns and activities.

The national network represents the entire movement of students involved in Acting on AIDS provides nationally organized events and campaigns such as the annual Student Leadership Summit. The program also provides interactive web tools and monthly conference calls as well as disseminate news to the collective network of students.

acting on AIDS

The intent of Acting on AIDS and the goal of this book is to encourage the younger generation of the church to respond to global issues as an expression of their discipleship as they come to understand God's love for His people. AIDS introduces many global issues and is both a product of injustice and catalyst for further inequities. The goal is to mobilize students, create a groundswell of activity, and bring attention to the AIDS pandemic and the injustices that feed it. Acting on AIDS introduces the fight against poverty, disease, and injustice as a journey toward understanding the life and message of Christ. This information may inspire you to make fighting injustice a manifestation of your relationship to God; it should not be taken as a message of despair about the state of AIDS and brokenness in the world. The purpose is not to focus on the problem, but to highlight the solutions that are found in knowing Christ and extending His hope towards others.

Acting on AIDS aims to equip students to become educators and advocates in the fight against AIDS. This book should be used to mobilize students to action. This generation will ultimately be held accountable for how it addresses this plague. Acting on AIDS' goal is larger than fighting AIDS—the goal is to extend the message of hope that Jesus offers.

what can you do?

When James, Lisa, and Jackie were confronted with the reality that AIDS is inflicting on millions of lives around the world, they were inspired to take action. How can you, as a college student, begin addressing the greatest humanitarian crisis of our time?

For starters, you can learn more about it. The book you hold in your hands is a great tool for getting started. Chapter 1 will give you the background of HIV and AIDS: what it is and how it spreads, how it developed into the pandemic it is today, what areas of the world are most affected, and who are its biggest victims. Chapter 2 will discuss the cultural practices and factors that contribute to the spread of HIV and how the vicious cycles of poverty, poor education, and government instability work together to compound the effects of this pandemic. Chapter 3 will tell you what's currently being done globally to prevent AIDS from spreading further, addressing medical, socio-economic, and cultural solutions. It will share what World Vision is doing to care for orphans and others who are left vulnerable. Finally, chapter 4 will tell you about more students who are making an impact in the fight against AIDS and, most importantly, tell you what you can do to get involved in fighting this global pandemic.

This is an action guide. The first part of the book is packed with information about countries and people around the world and how their lives are being forever altered by the AIDS pandemic. Pray through this first section; ask God to intervene on behalf of the victims, and ask how you can be used to care for His people who are suffering at the hands of AIDS. The final section of the book will give you several ideas for how you can take action to help raise awareness and advocate on behalf of those whose who are most affected by the disease. Ask God to show you how to step out in faith and respond to this crisis and to help you find others who will do the same.

— Jyl Hall
Manager, Acting on AIDS

Chapter 1

The World's Largest Health Challenge

spreading hope

In 2004, Nathaniel Elliot, a sophomore in high school went on a mission trip to Israel. While there, he learned that before his graduation in 2006, 40 million people would be infected with HIV. What started out for Nathaniel as a typical mission trip ended with him receiving a call from the Lord to try to change the way the younger generation of America responds to this deadly disease, particularly in Africa. "I was ignorant of the global impact of this disease," says Nathaniel. "I thought it was just a sexually transmitted disease. But to view it as something that is ravishing countries, innocent people, and demolishing economies had never crossed my mind before. I had to do something."

During the summer of 2006 Nathaniel and four friends traveled on a donated school bus across America visiting churches, youth groups, and conventions to challenge their generation to respond to this global crisis. Their tour, *Living Hope*, was a challenge to their peers: "It is no longer about these staggering statistics. It's about the face of a person. It's about real stories. You have to make this personal," says Nathaniel. This call is not only to increase awareness but to ask people to respond to a specific need. They raised more than $21,000 to help build a school in Africa through World Vision.

Nathaniel's passion and calling did not come to a halt in August with the end of the *Living Hope Tour*. When Nathaniel headed off to college in September, he made plans to partner with the Acting on AIDS chapter on his campus. One person willing to follow God's call to action can make a difference in the global fight against AIDS.

"A righteous man knows the rights of the poor; a wicked man does not understand such knowledge."
(Proverbs 29:7, ESV)

introduction to global AIDS

HIV is the most devastating disease of the 21st century. In the 14th century, the infamous bubonic plague took the lives of 35 million people. The joint United Nations Program on HIV/AIDS (UNAIDS) estimates that 3.1 million people died of AIDS in 2005, that 40.3 million people were living with HIV at the end of 2005, and that AIDS has killed more than 25 million people since the early 1980s.[1] The 65 million people who either have died or will die due to AIDS since the beginning of the pandemic is greater than the number of people killed by the bubonic plague[2] or the total number of civilian and military casualties in World War II.[3] The only pandemic to eclipse the death rates of AIDS was the Spanish influenza epidemic from 1918 to 1919. Experts estimate that it killed between 50 and 100 million people worldwide; that's between 2.8 and 5.6 percent of the global population at that time.[4]

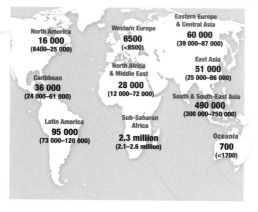

North America
16 000
(8400–25 000)

Western Europe
6500
(<8500)

Eastern Europe & Central Asia
60 000
(39 000–87 000)

North Africa & Middle East
28 000
(12 000–72 000)

East Asia
51 000
(25 000–86 000)

Caribbean
36 000
(24 000–61 000)

South & South-East Asia
490 000
(300 000–750 000)

Latin America
95 000
(73 000–120 000)

Sub-Saharan Africa
2.3 million
(2.1–2.6 million)

Oceania
700
(<1700)

Total: 3.1 (2.8–3.5) million

Estimated adult and child deaths due to HIV/AIDS during 2004

The AIDS pandemic's devastation reaches far beyond those who are infected. More than 15 million children worldwide have lost one or both parents to AIDS;[5] that number is expected to reach 25 million by the year 2010.[6] As AIDS is killing people in the prime of their lives, many children will grow up in communities with massive shortages of teachers, health care workers, civil servants, and business people. This perpetuates many of the vicious cycles of poverty that further the spread of HIV.

> More than 15 million children worldwide have lost one or both parents to AIDS; that number is expected to reach 25 million by the year 2010.

HIV/AIDS is the world's largest health challenge. And with a wide range of experts agreeing that problems associated with AIDS will dominate the 21st century, it is clear that young people today will inherit a world devastated by AIDS.

In this chapter, you will learn what HIV and AIDS are, how HIV is transmitted, and how it destroys a person's immune system. You will also learn about the history of the disease and how it was discovered. Then, you will see how this pandemic looks in specific regions across the world.

the basics—what is HIV?

H uman — Infects men, women, and children regardless of race or age.

I mmunodeficiency — Destroys the human body's natural ability to fight infections.

V irus — Small, infectious agent that reproduces within a person.

HIV is the virus that gradually damages the body's immune system and eventually causes AIDS. The human body is equipped with CD4 cells, also called helper T cells, which defend the body against viruses and bacteria. HIV damages the immune system by attacking and entering these cells. Once inside the cells, the viruses reproduce and then move on to attack other helper T cells and repeat the process. As more helper T cells are overtaken, the body becomes less and less able to fight off illnesses.

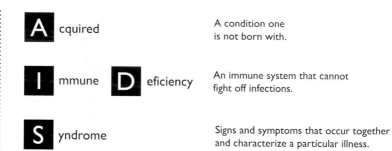

A person can be infected with the virus for three to five years—and sometimes as many as 10 years—without knowing it or feeling sick.

A person can be infected with the virus for three to five years—and sometimes as many as 10 years—without knowing it or feeling sick. Despite the appearance of good health, the person is able to spread the virus and, without treatment, will ultimately develop AIDS.

what is AIDS?

A cquired

A condition one is not born with.

I mmune **D** eficiency

An immune system that cannot fight off infections.

S yndrome

Signs and symptoms that occur together and characterize a particular illness.

When one's immune system is so damaged that it cannot fight "opportunistic" infections—infections healthy immune systems can fight off but weakened ones can't—he or she is said to have AIDS. Because the body is not able to fight off these diseases, the person will eventually die. The most common opportunistic infections include tuberculosis, pneumonia, skin cancer, meningitis, thrush, herpes, and bacterial infections that cause fevers, digestive difficulties, and weight loss. AIDS manifests itself differently in every individual. Some people die very soon after becoming infected, while others may live for a decade or more without treatment.

Bodily Fluids

HIV is transmitted when a person has contact with certain bodily fluids of another person who is HIV-positive.

Bodily fluids that can contain and transmit HIV include:

- Blood
- Wound discharge or pus
- Semen
- Vaginal fluid
- Breast milk

Bodily fluids that can contain and transmit HIV, which medical staff may contact, include:

- Fluid surrounding the brain and spinal cord
- Fluid surrounding bone joints
- Fluid surrounding an unborn baby

HIV is primarily transmitted in the following ways:

Sexual Activity

Sexual activity is the most common form of HIV transmission. HIV can be transmitted through any kind of sexual activity (vaginal, anal, and oral) and can occur when bodily fluids of an HIV-positive partner enter into the other partner, including through small, even unidentifiable, cuts or scratches.

Women, and especially girls, are twice as vulnerable as men to contracting HIV through sexual activity due to their biological and physiological characteristics.

Women, and especially girls, are twice as vulnerable as men to contract HIV through sexual activity due to their biological and physiological characteristics. This vulnerability rises substantially in cases of coercive and/or violent sexual intercourse.

Sexually Transmitted Infections

The risk of transmission is further increased if either partner has a sexually transmitted infection (STI). An STI is any disease that is passed from one person to another through sexual contact, such as chlamydia, genital herpes, genital warts, gonorrhea, and syphilis. HIV is also an STI.

A person with an STI is 10 times more likely to transmit or acquire HIV than a person without an STI because (1) many STIs cause open sores or breaks in the skin, providing an avenue for HIV to enter the body, and (2) the bodily fluids of individuals with STIs have an increased concentration of helper T cells, which serve as targets for HIV and may increase the risk of infection.

A person with an STI is 10 times more likely to transmit HIV or acquire HIV than a person without an STI.

Symptoms of STIs include:

• Open sores or breaks in the skin around the genitals

• White, yellow, or green vaginal discharge

• Burning sensation when passing urine

• Itchiness in the genital area

• Pain in the lower stomach or back

• Pain in the testicles

• Pain during sexual activity

Some STIs, however, have no symptoms. (Thus, it is important to visit a health clinic for proper diagnosis and treatment if you think there is a possibility that you've been exposed.) Most STIs are curable. Left untreated, STIs—in addition to facilitating the transmission of HIV—can lead to serious complications, including infertility and cervical cancer.

Blood Transfusions

An individual can become infected if he or she is given HIV-infected blood during a blood transfusion. Most countries now test donated blood for HIV, making the risk low. However, in situations where such screening is not done, the risk is much higher.

Sharing Needles or Using Syringes and Razor Blades

Needles, syringes, razor blades, and other instruments that pierce the skin (for drug injection, tattooing, piercing, carving scars, circumcision, or shaving) can transmit the virus if they were used first by an infected person. One can even contract HIV in a health-care setting if syringes, needles, and equipment are not properly sterilized.

Mother-to-Child Transmission

An HIV-infected woman can pass the virus to her baby during pregnancy through the placenta and during childbirth through exposure to the mother's blood. Without treatment, approximately 15–30% of babies born to HIV-positive mothers are infected with the virus. HIV also can be transmitted to a breast-feeding baby through the mother's milk. Breast-feeding by an HIV-positive mother increases the risk of transmission to her baby by 10–20%.[7] Antiretroviral preventive treatment is an effective method of preventing mother-to-child transmission of HIV. When combined with the use of safer infant-feeding methods, it can halve the risk of infant infection.

False Transmitters

HIV is not acquired through the following:

- Living in the same place with people who have HIV/AIDS
- Kissing (unless there are open sores or exposure to blood within the mouth)
- Touch (hugging, hand-shaking, or sports contact)
- Bites from mosquitoes or other insects
- Shared food, utensils, cups, or dishes

- Shared swimming pools or bathing facilities
- Sneezes or coughs
- Hospital visits
- Sweat, saliva, or tears*
- Urine or feces*

* Research indicates that HIV can be found in these substances, but in too low of a concentration for transmission.

phases of the disease from HIV Infection to AIDS

HIV Infection

Once people are infected with HIV, they may experience cold or influenza-like symptoms—including fever and swollen glands in the neck, underarms, and groin—within a month or two. This is called the "acute phase." Once these symptoms subside, they could live many years without experiencing symptoms associated with AIDS. During this time, they may not know they are infected or appear sick. However, they are able to spread the virus to others who come in contact with their bodily fluids. A person's appearance cannot be used as an indicator of whether or not one is HIV-positive.

Early Stages of AIDS

Eventually HIV infection progresses so that more obvious signs of sickness begin to appear. The first symptoms can be any of the following:

- Weight loss (greater than 10% of body weight)
- Lack of energy
- Chronic diarrhea lasting longer than one month
- Chronic cough lasting longer than one month
- Painful sores or rashes
- Sores on the lips that do not heal

- Fevers and night sweats
- Swollen glands in neck, armpits, and groin (very soon after infection)
- Thrush (a white rash) in the mouth or on the genitals
- Repeated infections in throat or ears
- Recurring shingles

Late Stages of AIDS

People living with AIDS can develop any of these opportunistic infections or symptoms:

- Respiratory conditions such as atypical tuberculosis and severe recurrent pneumonia
- Further weight loss
- Extreme fatigue
- Dark-blue or reddish-brown marks on the skin (known as Kaposi's Sarcoma)
- Painful and itchy skin rashes
- Prickly pain in the hands and feet
- Thrush (a white rash) in the mouth or on the genitals
- Mental disorders, such as dementia, resulting from infections in the brain

the history of HIV and AIDS

The Discovery of HIV and AIDS

HIV and AIDS appeared in the late 1970s when doctors began to see an increasing number of patients with an unusual strain of pneumonia and rare cancers. Some noticed the disease appeared most often in men who had sex with men and began calling it Gay-Related Immune Deficiency Syndrome or GRID. The Human Immunodeficiency Virus

(HIV) was isolated in 1983 by Luc Montagnier at the French Institute Pasteur. This virus was called Lymphadenopathy-Associated Virus. Not long after, Robert Gallo of the U.S. National Cancer Institute discovered a related virus he called HTLV-3.

> AIDS was clinically identified in 1983, but medical experts believe the syndrome existed for many years before it was recognized.

AIDS was clinically identified in 1983, but medical experts believe the syndrome existed for many years before it was recognized, evidenced by clusters of people infected with what may have been AIDS in a number of places in southern and eastern Africa.

Initial Perceptions within the United States

When the first cases of AIDS were reported in the United States, some of the best medical minds went to work on the problem. After a period of time, blood supplies were tested and purged of potentially infected blood. "At-risk" populations were urged to seek HIV testing. Because the homosexual community was originally the hardest hit, this well-educated and well-resourced segment of the population brought considerable attention to the problem. Due to this, most people in the United States quickly learned about AIDS and how it is transmitted.[8]

> Nearly 500,000 individuals have died of AIDS in the United States. However, the rate of infection has decreased by 70% since 1994.

Nearly 500,000 individuals have died of AIDS in the United States. However, the rate of infection has decreased by 70% since 1994. Many who are HIV-positive are also benefiting from drug therapies that have prolonged their lives and increased their quality of life.

While the United States' highest HIV incidence has been in the homosexual community, in much of the rest of the world HIV is transmitted primarily through heterosexual sex, intravenous drug use, transmission from infected mothers to their babies, and infection through the blood supply.[9]

AIDS around the World

Whereas a common misconception in the past was that AIDS is a homosexual disease, today the disease is more commonly misperceived as an African one. While it is true that more than 25 million people in Africa are living with HIV or AIDS,[10] it is a mistake to judge HIV/AIDS as an "African problem."[11] Epidemics are growing in regions all over the globe, with Eastern Europe and Central Asia actually experiencing the largest percentage of new infections—nearly a twenty-fold increase in less than 10 years. As the disease continues to reach far deeper than any one continent or people group, the world has begun to recognize that AIDS is a global problem needing a global response.

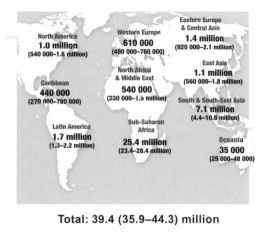

North America
1.0 million
(540 000–1.6 million)

Western Europe
610 000
(480 000–760 000)

Eastern Europe
& Central Asia
1.4 million
(920 000–2.1 million)

Caribbean
440 000
(270 000–780 000)

North Africa
& Middle East
540 000
(230 000–1.5 million)

East Asia
1.1 million
(560 000–1.8 million)

South & South-East Asia
7.1 million
(4.4–10.6 million)

Latin America
1.7 million
(1.3–2.2 million)

Sub-Saharan
Africa
25.4 million
(23.4–28.4 million)

Oceania
35 000
(25 000–48 000)

Total: 39.4 (35.9–44.3) million

Adults and children estimated to be living with HIV/AIDS as of the end of 2004

> *While is true that more than 25 million people in Africa are living with HIV or AIDS, it is a mistake to judge HIV and AIDS as an "African problem."*

The annual AIDS death toll of 3 million people has been compared to twenty fully loaded 747 airplanes crashing every day for a year.[12] Reported cases of AIDS are rising so swiftly in China and India that if nothing is done, the death rates there will eclipse the numbers being reported in Africa.[13] Most estimates show that the AIDS infection rate

North America
44 000
(16 000–120 000)

Caribbean
53 000
(27 000–140 000)

Latin America
240 000
(170 000–430 000)

Western Europe
21 000
(14 000–38 000)

North Africa
& Middle East
92 000
(34 000–350 000)

Sub-Saharan
Africa
3.1 million
(2.7–3.8 million)

Eastern Europe
& Central Asia
210 000
(110 000–480 000)

East Asia
290 000
(84 000–830 000)

South & South-East Asia
890 000
(480 000–2.0 million)

Oceania
5 000
(2100–13 000)

Total: 4.9 (4.3–6.4) million

Estimated number of adults and children newly infected with HIV during 2004

and death toll will continue to grow rapidly until at least 2010, even with aggressive worldwide interventions.

Sub-Saharan Africa

Sub-Saharan Africa is home to less than 10% of the world's population but has 60% of all people living with HIV and AIDS. Southern Africa remains the epicenter of the global AIDS pandemic. For many years, before the isolation of the HIV virus in the early 1980s, many Africans used the term "slim" to refer to the condition later known as AIDS, because the disease caused them to waste away until death. Many in Africa still use this term to refer to those who are living with AIDS.

Because of sub-Saharan Africa's high HIV infection rate, many experts agree that AIDS probably spread from this region. The long-term presence of killer diseases such as malaria, tuberculosis, and dysentery could have initially masked the existence of AIDS.[14]

Because of sub-Saharan Africa's high HIV infection rate, many experts agree that AIDS probably spread from this region.

Even after HIV was identified, African countries have continued to struggle to address the epidemic, largely because public health facilities are poor, communication systems are fragmented, and many governments are unstable.

Transmission of HIV in Africa happens primarily through heterosexual activity. Even today, much of the population still does not understand how HIV is transmitted, and infection rates cannot be accurately collected in Africa's highly rural, poor countries.

The good news is that the prevalence of HIV in adults appears to be declining in three sub-Saharan African countries: Kenya, Uganda, and Zimbabwe. Some of this decline can be attributed to changes in sexual behavior.[15] Reasons for this will be discussed in chapter 3.

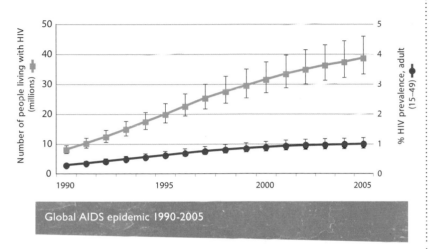

Global AIDS epidemic 1990-2005

Asia

In many Asian countries, the percentage of the population that is HIV-positive is low compared with many countries in sub-Saharan Africa. Yet, because populations are large in many Asian countries, even a low prevalence rate means large numbers of people are infected. In 2005, 8.3 million Asian adults and children were living with HIV—1.1 million of these became infected just that year.[16] India has already surpassed South Africa as having the highest number of people living with HIV in the world, with more than 5.7 million people infected as of 2005.[17]

India has already surpassed South Africa as having the highest number of people living with HIV in the world, with more than 5.7 million people infected as of 2005.

> The Caribbean is the second most affected region of the world after sub-Saharan Africa, with 24,000 adult and child deaths due to AIDS in 2005.

Risky behavior feeds the AIDS epidemics in Asia. The interplay of intravenous drug use and unprotected sex—much of it transactional sex—fuels its spread. In China, for example, AIDS is prevalent among intravenous drug users, sex workers, and former plasma donors. Because the majority of drug injectors are sexually active and large portions of them also buy or sell sex, the pandemic can spread quickly.

Indonesia, Vietnam, and China are most at risk for widespread infection. Unless these and several other Asian countries implement programs designed to limit HIV transmission among at-risk groups, HIV is expected to continue its unrelenting march across much of the Asian continent.[18]

Eastern Europe and Central Asia

In 2005, the number of people living with HIV in this region reached an estimated 1.6 million—a twenty-fold increase in less than 10 years. Compared to 2003, AIDS claimed nearly twice as many lives in 2005, killing an estimated 62,000 adults and children. The most affected countries in this region are Russia and Ukraine. The epidemics in both of these countries are fueled by risky sexual behavior and prevalent intravenous drug use among young people. In Russia up to 40% of all drug injectors use non-sterile needles or syringes. Several Central Asian and Caucasian republics are seeing the early stages of high infection rates, and high levels of risky behavior could broaden the epidemic in southeastern Europe.[19]

Latin America and the Caribbean

The Caribbean is the second most affected region of the world after sub-Saharan Africa, with 24,000 adult and child deaths due to AIDS in 2005.[20] The region's epidemic is driven primarily by sex, with commercial sex playing a significant role in the spread of HIV. Social conditions, such as severe poverty, high unemployment, and gender inequality, contribute to an environment ripe for the pandemic's growth. For example, in Trinidad and Tobago, HIV infection levels are six times higher among 15- to-19-year-old females than among males of the same age. This trend is largely caused by the common practice of older men establishing relationships with younger women.

Brazil alone accounts for more than one-third of the estimated 1.8 million people living with HIV in Latin America. However, the highest prevalence is found in the smaller countries of Belize, Guatemala, and Honduras. Like in other areas of the world, the epidemic in this region is being fed by both unsafe sex and intravenous drug use. In nearly all Latin American countries, the highest levels of HIV infection are found among men who have sex with men, and the second-highest levels are among female sex workers. In 2005, 66,000 adults and children died due to AIDS, and 200,000 were newly infected.[21]

Western/Central Europe and North America

The number of people living with HIV in these regions rose to 1.9 million in 2005, up from 1.8 million in 2003. In both years, 30,000 adults and children died due to AIDS. Wide availability of antiretroviral therapy has helped keep AIDS deaths comparatively low. Most of the individuals living with HIV in the United States are men who have sex with men.[22]

Studies show African Americans also have disproportionate infection rates. Despite constituting only 12.5% of the country's population, African Americans accounted for 48% of new HIV cases in 2003. By some estimates, African American women are 12 times as likely to be infected with HIV as their white counterparts. African Americans also appear to be half as likely to receive antiretroviral drugs. For women living with HIV, unsafe heterosexual intercourse is the main mode of transmission. For many HIV-positive women, the main risk factor for acquiring the virus remains the often-undisclosed risk behavior of male partners, such as intravenous drug use and sex with other men.[23]

Despite constituting only 12.5% of the country's population, African Americans accounted for 48% of new HIV cases in 2003.

In Canada, the number of annually reported new HIV infections has risen 20% since 2000. In Western Europe, more than half-a-million people are living with HIV. The most common trend throughout Western Europe is the steadily growing proportion of newly diagnosed HIV infections due to unsafe heterosexual intercourse, but sex between men remains a notable factor in the epidemics in Belgium, Denmark, Switzerland, and Germany.[24]

Western Europe and North America remain the only parts of the world where most people in need of antiretroviral treatment are able to receive it. As a result, the number of AIDS deaths plummeted in the late 1990s. In contrast, Eastern Europe—where antiretroviral treatment availability is limited—the number of AIDS deaths has tripled since 2000.[25]

conclusion

At this point, you should have a basic understanding of HIV and AIDS. This chapter has discussed what this virus is, how it is transmitted, and how HIV and AIDS attack one's immune system. It also reviewed how this pandemic reaches far beyond age, gender, and ethnicity.

Much of the information found in this book will be surprising when AIDS is seen through the lens of the global issues that are perpetuating this disease. The following chapters will discuss how structural injustices and poor choices are creating vicious cycles, allowing for the rapid spread of HIV and AIDS. This book will also discuss how to break those cycles by addressing these inequities and by empowering healthy choices.

an orphan and a parent

Theoneste was only 16 when his mother died—a traumatic experience for any teenager. Yet his grief was compounded by the fact that his mother was the only adult in the family. With her death, he faced an unwelcome launch into a new stage in life: parenthood. It was now his responsibility to care for his three siblings, ages 9 to 15.

After their mother's death, the children lived with their elderly grandmother until an uncle came to visit and kicked them out of the house. For five months they wandered the community, sleeping wherever someone would let them. World Vision learned of the children's plight and built them a three-bedroom house with locking doors and windows, a latrine, and a separate cooking building—all next door to their grandmother's house.

Theoneste, 17, and his sister Josee, 9, sit on the bed they share with their other two siblings.

However, even with a new house, life is not easy. While World Vision also provides the children with educational fees so they can attend school, goats to provide fertilizer for the garden behind the house, and extra food, there never seems to be enough. Each day, the children hurry along the two-mile route from school to their home to finish their chores before dark. One cooks, another gathers wood, still another carries water. When the chores are finished, there is homework to be done.

AIDS doesn't affect just one family—Theoneste's neighbors also know what it is like to lose a loved one or friend to AIDS.

The children consider themselves blessed to have one meal a day. At times, Theoneste is afraid he will have to quit school to earn an income. Yet he will not give up hope. "If God wishes," he said, "I will be able to finish my studies, get a job, and support my younger brother and sisters so they can finish school, too."

discussion questions

Q In what ways have you come in contact with the AIDS pandemic? Have you seen movies or read books on AIDS? Discuss some of these and what they have taught you about this issue. In what ways do you think their portrayal is accurate? How has AIDS affected you personally?

Q As you read through the first few sections on the basics of HIV and how it is transmitted, did you learn anything new? What about the list of "False Transmitters"? Were you surprised by any of the ways the disease is, or is not, spread?

Q This chapter discusses how perceptions have changed throughout the history of AIDS. What was once thought of as a homosexual problem is now conceived of as mostly an African problem. What are the reasons for these perceptions, and how might they be harmful?

Q As you reflect on the ways AIDS is affecting different regions around the world, what are some of the patterns you see? What are the common cultural denominators that affect how quickly it is spread? What do the countries with the highest infection and AIDS-related death rates have in common? What do the countries with the lowest infection and AIDS-related death rates have in common?

action items

1. Nathaniel Elliot, the student described in the beginning of this chapter, felt called to give up his last summer before college to make a difference in the fight against AIDS. After his tour, he joined the Acting on AIDS chapter on his college campus to stay involved in the fight. Is there an Acting on AIDS chapter on your campus? If so, find a way to get involved in what they're doing. If not, look into to starting one on your campus. (See chapter 4 for more information on starting your own Acting on AIDS chapter.)

2. If you or someone you know is involved in behavior that puts you or them at risk of contracting HIV, such as risky sexual relationships or sharing needles with someone who has HIV/AIDS, the only way to avoid contracting the virus is to stop. Everyone involved should get tested for HIV. Also, find someone with

whom you can talk about this, someone who will help you or your friend give up these practices and encourage you or your friend to stay safe.

3. The most important action step is to pray. Go back through the different areas of the world and pray against the cultural and economic realities of the countries with the highest HIV infection rates. Pray for those already involved in the fight against AIDS, and ask God to bless their efforts to treat the victims, educate others, or advocate on behalf of those suffering from AIDS. Ask that God would help doctors and scientists discover new treatments for helping people who are living with HIV or AIDS. Pray that more and more people would respond to this global pandemic and come into a deeper understanding of the call to care for the poor and diseased as a response to the life of Jesus.

4. How can you encourage your church to care for those affected by HIV and AIDS? How can you encourage others in your community to care for widows and orphans?

Chapter 2

Symptoms of a Broken World

role call

What do you see yourself doing in one year? Four years? How about 10 years? What role will you be playing? Can this role be integrated with the fight against HIV and AIDS?

Lindsey Schmidt, a graduate student at Geneva College, wants to make a contribution. But not long ago she was neither aware of the seriousness of the AIDS pandemic nor considering integrating her career with this issue. While interning at World Vision in Pittsburgh, she became aware of this crisis but had no idea what to do about it.

Then Lindsey learned about Acting on AIDS. Inspired and feeling called to respond, Lindsey and fellow students brought Acting on AIDS to their campus and rallied Geneva's community around this issue. "It is my problem," says Lindsey. "I feel a weight and a burden for those infected with and affected by HIV and AIDS. . . . I feel that HIV and AIDS should be one of the primary issues of my generation, the church, and the world. We will be judged by future generations by how we handled the HIV and AIDS pandemic. There is something wrong when a disease that is 100 percent preventable is killing our world, our brothers and sisters, each one of us."

After two years of advising the Acting on AIDS chapter leadership, she felt called to incorporate her master's in higher education to study the ways students are responding to the AIDS pandemic. Lindsey has challenged her peers and her campus community to become involved with global issues. "College students are in the perfect position to effect change in the world. Once students are educated about global

AIDS, they are capable of influencing others by sharing information with them." Lindsey's role is defined as an activist, educator, and leader. What will yours be?

"Once again old men and women will walk Jerusalem's streets with a cane and sit together in the city squares. And the streets of the city will be filled with boys and girls at play." This is what the LORD Almighty says: "All this may seem impossible to you now, a small and discouraged remnant of God's people. But do you think this is impossible for me, the LORD Almighty?" This is what the LORD Almighty says: "You can be sure that I will rescue my people. " (Zechariah 8: 4–7, NLT)

those suffering in a broken world

In many of the countries most devastated by AIDS, there are already severe injustices in place that limit people's access to education and their ability to provide a living, and threaten their basic human rights. Sadly, the people who are most threatened by these injustices— women, orphans, and the poor—are also disproportionately affected by the AIDS crisis.

Women

A girl born today in a poor community becomes part of the largest group of people to be denied basic needs and human rights: women. The second-class status of women have in many poor and developing countries is also seen in the AIDS pandemic. Physiological and cultural factors put women at a greater risk for contracting HIV. Physiologically, women are more likely to contract HIV through a single exposure because the cervix is particularly vulnerable to infection—especially from abrasions caused by violent or forced sex. Culturally, women are often socially marginalized, denied basic legal rights and education, and vulnerable to physical and sexual abuse.

Among 15- to 24-year-olds, there are six times more women than men living with HIV in some African countries.

In sub-Saharan Africa, close to 60% of adults living with HIV and AIDS—a total of 13.3 million people—are women. Among 15- to 24-year-olds, there are six times more women than men living with HIV in some African countries. In the past two years, East Asia has seen a 56% increase in the number of women infected with HIV, and Europe and Central Asia were not far behind with a 48% increase in infection rates in women over the same period of time.[1]

A girl may be given less food, denied urgent medical care, and assigned exhausting chores. She may be forced to end her education to marry early, to care for a sick parent, or to provide for the family. Also, when women marry, they are often left without basic legal documentation and rights. In many developing countries, women's inheritance and property rights are not enforced, and many women marry without a marriage certificate, making their claims difficult to prove to the authorities. This lack of property rights, coupled with a lack of education, gives many women few options if they are widowed or divorced.

Women are also substantially less likely to be educated in developing countries. Across 131 developing countries in four major regions, there is a pervasive literacy gap of 8.8%, on average, between men and women.[2] Literate women are three times more likely than illiterate women to know that a healthy-looking person can have HIV, and

Srey Mom, 17, was tricked into entering a brothel when she was 13, where she contracted HIV. World Vision reunited her with her family, provided her medication, and gave her tools with which to earn a living.

four times more likely to know the main ways to avoid AIDS.[3] In Zimbabwe, one study found that girls between 15 and 18 who had dropped out of school were six times more likely to be living with HIV than girls who were still in school.[4]

Madhu and her siblings were orphaned by AIDS. Madhu, 17, lives in India in Guntur district with her sister, 13, and two brothers, 15 and 11.

In many developing countries, women's relationships are marked by violence, coercion, and economic dependency. Spousal abuse, which is endemic in many countries, can discourage wives from confronting their husbands about extra-marital affairs or asking them to use a condom when they have sex. Negative cultural practices like female genital mutilation and widow cleansing[5] (a cultural practice in some communities in Africa and Asia where a woman is essentially raped in her home by men of the village to "cleanse" her from her husband's death) violently take away a woman's ability to protect herself from being infected with HIV. Also, in contexts where women and girls are afraid of being abused or are forced out of their homes if they are HIV-positive, they may put off testing or treatment out of fear of being discovered.

Orphans and Vulnerable Children

Children orphaned or vulnerable due to AIDS are less likely to be educated than other children. They are more likely to be malnourished, more vulnerable to abuse and exploitation, and more likely to suffer from depression. An orphan is defined as a child who has lost one or both parents. Vulnerable children are those living with chronically ill parents, children living in households fostering orphans, or any other children who meet the definition of extreme poverty in their communities.

Orphans and vulnerable children (OVC) are less likely to be educated, often because they are unable to pay school fees, must work to survive, or are discriminated against in a foster household.[6] Data from Demographic and Health Surveys from 20 countries in Africa, Latin America, and the Caribbean found that among children aged 10 to 14, 77% of non-orphaned children attended school, while only 56% of orphaned children were enrolled.[7] Another study found that children who had lost both parents dropped out of school at nearly twice the rate (17.1%) as children whose parents were living (9.5%) during the 2000 school year.[8]

Orphans and vulnerable children are more likely than other children to be malnourished or hungry. Households affected by HIV and AIDS have been shown in some contexts to experience a drop in food consumption of more than 40%. Data from Lesotho found that the proportion of underweight orphaned children aged 0 to 4 years is almost double that of non-orphaned children.[9] Furthermore, OVC are often subject to physical, sexual, and emotional abuse at the hands of foster families, community members, and even other children.

> Households affected by HIV and AIDS have been shown in some contexts to experience a drop in food consumption of more than 40%.

The trauma of watching parents grow ill and die, being separated from siblings, and possibly being abused or neglected can cause deep emotional scarring in children. One study in Uganda found that the average score for orphans on the Childhood Depression Index was 19.0, above the 18.0 cut-off for clinical depression, while the average score for non-orphans was 12.0.[10]

These circumstances—all of which also make OVC more likely to live in poverty as adults—can seriously limit their ability to make healthy decisions to avoid contracting HIV themselves. Orphaned adolescents in Zambia are much more likely—23.1% versus 15.7%—to engage in risky sexual behavior than other children.[11] Orphans and children living with chronically ill caregivers are more likely than other children to consume alcohol—a major risk factor for unsafe sexual behavior. In other words, orphans and vulnerable children may, as a group, be more likely to contract HIV, which will further increase the population of orphans and vulnerable children.

Formerly abducted child soldiers play with a wooden gun used in reenactment dramas, which are part of rehabilitation therapy sessions. Many are familiar with how to handle the weapon. This picture was taken at World Vision's Children of War Rehabilitation Center in Gulu, Uganda.

Child Soldiers

In countries with unstable governments or civil wars, orphans are more vulnerable to the exploitation of rebel leaders and warlords who wish to recruit them into their armies—often through abduction and intimidation. Orphans living on the street or in child-headed households are often prime targets for these tactics. Some, in the most desperate of circumstances, may join these groups willingly, searching for acceptance and purpose.

Children cost less to train and feed, making them the military equivalent of "cheap labor." In the Liberian civil war, Charles Taylor turned a core group of 150 fighters into a force of several thousand through the enlistment of children as combatants.[12] In Sierra Leone, it is estimated that 6,000 children fought in that country's civil war on both sides, with children between the ages of 7 and 14 making up a significant percentage of the Rebel United Front forces.[13] During the last 20 years of Uganda's civil war, at least 30,000 children have been kidnapped and forced to be soldiers, laborers, and sexual slaves in the rebel Lord's Resistance Army.[14] Child soldiers are quickly replaceable due to the cruel simplicity of their recruitment, indoctrination, and training.

vicious cycles

Many of the countries that have been most traumatized by the AIDS pandemic are battling critical problems like drugs, poor educational systems, inadequate food supplies, insufficient health care systems, and unstable governments. When combined with the additional problem of AIDS, vicious cycles are created as these problems feed off each other and create a vortex that threatens to bring down whole communities or even countries. These cycles and problems must be understood and addressed by any efforts to combat the AIDS crisis.

Food Scarcity

HIV and AIDS contribute to problems of hunger and food shortages. Less people mean less labor for the production of food. AIDS has already killed 7 million farmers in Africa since 1985, and it could kill 16 million more by 2020. Namibia is projected to lose 26% of its agricultural labor force. Other states are similarly affected, including Botswana (23%), Zimbabwe (23%), Mozambique (20%), South Africa (20%), Kenya (17%), Malawi (14%), Uganda (14%), and Tanzania (13%).[15]

Rural families affected by HIV and AIDS often have to reduce the amount of land they cultivate and shift the diversity of their crops from high-value, labor intensive, cash crops to a few basic cereal grains. One study in Mozambique found that 45% of AIDS-affected households had reduced the area of land they cultivated, and 60% had reduced the number of crops grown.[16]

Ethiopian households affected by HIV and AIDS spent just 12 to 16 hours per week on farming, compared to 34 hours per week for households not affected by HIV and AIDS.[17] Often these households are forced to sell any remaining assets, deplete savings, and go into debt to pay for medical expenses and funeral costs. Other productive assets, such as irrigation and grain storage systems, often fall into disrepair.

Widows and children orphaned by AIDS are often the victims of property grabbing, which robs them of the land they need to grow food. A Ugandan study reported that 29% of widows, and 20% of teenage orphans have had property seized by outsiders.[18]

While HIV and AIDS help create food insecurity, food insecurity helps to drive the spread of HIV and AIDS. Hunger increases the likelihood that people will adopt risky strategies to survive. Men may migrate to find work, and women and children may turn to prostitution to earn money for food, which drastically increases the risk of HIV infection. A study in Tanzania found that one-quarter of elementary school girls surveyed said they had engaged in sex with adult men, including their teachers, in exchange for money. [19]

Malaria and HIV

Malaria is the world's most prevalent tropical parasitic disease. It exacts an enormous toll in lives, medical costs, and lost labor. It is estimated that malaria has cost Africa $100 billion dollars over the last 30 years.[20] Ninety percent of all malaria deaths occur in Africa, and malaria is one of the biggest killers of children under 5.[21]

The interaction between malaria and HIV is now being uncovered. Together, they cause more than 4 million deaths per year. Malaria infection is more frequent and more severe in HIV-positive pregnant women, and malaria may contribute to increased HIV viral loads in those who are HIV-positive.[22] This could explain the increased transmission of HIV and the more rapid disease progression found in Africa. According to a recent report by the World Health Organization, "Malaria and HIV/AIDS are both diseases of poverty and causes of poverty, and they share determinants of vulnerability. Given the wide geographic overlap in oc-

Migrant workers often work long hours in poor, sometimes dangerous, conditions and live in environments that are devoid of healthy relationships, community, or positive ways to de-stress after a long day.

currence and the resulting co-infection, the interaction between the two diseases clearly has major public health implications."[23]

The most widely used, low-cost anti-malarial drugs are now useless in many places due to widespread resistance. The mosquito, the vector of the malarial parasite, is showing increasing resistance to many insecticides. Better anti-malarial drugs for sub-Saharan Africa and insecticide-treated nets for people suffering from HIV and AIDS are desperately needed.

Migration and Mobility

Migration is a huge factor in issues of poverty and the spread of the disease. In areas with low economic growth and high unemployment, men and women often leave their communities to find work elsewhere.

Migrant workers often work long hours in poor, sometimes dangerous, conditions and live in environments that are devoid of healthy relationships,

These three girls have been trafficked into Cambodia from Vietnam. They are prostitutes in an area called "The Street of Little Flowers." The brothel across the street is known to employ girls as young as 12 and 13 years old.

community, or positive ways to de-stress after a long day. As a result, many choose drinking and risky sexual encounters to relieve their stress and loneliness.

Throughout Africa and Asia, large numbers of truck drivers, bus drivers, and other mobile workers visit sex workers while they are away from their families. In Cambodia, there are almost 200 brothels along the most heavily trafficked sections of major national highways. In southern and eastern Africa, trucking routes can be extremely dangerous and customs inspection at border crossings can take days, causing truck drivers to sit idle while their trucks are being inspected. Away from their families, living in precarious safety while on the road in poor nations, and sitting around bored for days on end, truck drivers gravitate to the bars and brothels. Border crossing towns, and many towns along the major trucking routes in Africa, are among the most hopeless places on earth.

Substance Abuse and Trafficking

Addiction to drugs and alcohol are major factors that can cause people to make risky choices. Alcohol and drug abuse are commonly linked to high-risk sexual behavior and the sharing of HIV-contaminated needles and syringes. All of these activities contribute to the spread of HIV.

Some environmental factors make people more susceptible to drug and alcohol addiction in the first place. One such factor is drug trafficking. In Central Asia, Russia, Eastern Europe, China, Southeast Asia, and many other places around major drug production centers, drug trafficking produces drug addiction and leads to the spread of HIV and AIDS. The presence of large amounts of drugs and narco-trafficking money drives down the price of drugs and makes them accessible to more people.

Poor Education

AIDS is affecting the educational prospects of children in poor countries by reducing the number of enrolled students, reducing the number of skilled teachers, and contributing to gender inequality. This will have severe consequences: uneducated children are more than twice as likely to contract HIV than those who have completed primary education.[24]

In Zambia and Zimbabwe, the number of children who are enrolling and graduating from primary school has dropped significantly. Secondary schools do not have the capacity to enroll all of the students who do graduate from primary school. In Tanzania, only 41,238 (9.7%) of 426,562 students who graduated from primary school in 1999 were selected to enroll in public secondary school.[25] In Uganda, there were only 179,305 secondary school spots available in 2003 for the 485,703 students who had graduated from primary school in 2002.[26]

One study suggests that South Africa will need to train 30,000 new teachers each year by 2010, roughly six times the current number trained annually.

While the number of students who are able to attend school declines, the number of teachers who are healthy and able to teach is decreasing as well. The World Bank estimates that the HIV prevalence rate among highly skilled primary and secondary school teachers is roughly equivalent to that in the general population, meaning that 24.6% of teachers in Zimbabwe, 14.2% in Malawi, 12.2% in Mozambique, and 5.1% in Rwanda may be living with HIV and AIDS.[27] Many governments are not able to train teachers fast enough to keep up with the number of teachers who are dying from AIDS. One study suggests that South Africa will need to train 30,000 new teachers each year by 2010, roughly six times the current number trained annually.[28]

Ramkamni is a 7-year-old boy living with HIV. He and his family are cared for by World Vision's Hope Care Centre in northeast India.

The number of girls who have access to education is dropping due to the AIDS pandemic. In many poor families, boys are sent to school instead of their female siblings. Girls may be needed to help at home, and families often cannot afford the cost of sending multiple children to school. Often, girls are locked into the social assumption that their education is less important because they are expected to marry and care for a family.

Unstable Environments

Emergency situations that are either caused by man (such as war) or by nature (such as natural disasters) can exacerbate the problems of poverty, powerlessness, and social instability. These factors greatly increase the risk of HIV transmission. Although the problems of war and natural disasters are unrelated in cause, their impact on communities can be similar.

Children flock to the Noah's Ark shelter in Gulu, Uganda, to avoid abduction from the Lord's Resistance Army. Up to 1,000 children a night seek shelter here, and thousands more walk to other shelters in the area.

Quick-onset emergencies lead to heightened vulnerability for all people. In such unstable environments, women and girls will often be exposed to sexual violence in the form of rape and other abuse, particularly where rape is used as a weapon of war. And the further impoverishment that accompanies crisis situations may lead women to acts of desperation, such as resorting to commercial and transactional sex in order to provide for themselves and their children. For men and boys, the sexual norms of the military, as well as increased vulnerabilities from displacement or labor migration, promote risky sexual behavior and bring a higher risk of contracting HIV. In high HIV-prevalence areas, recovery from emergencies takes much longer if there is not specific help directed to households affected by HIV and AIDS.

Stigma and Discrimination

If you are in a community that stigmatizes HIV and AIDS and are suspected of being HIV-positive, people may stop talking to you and stop buying your goods. Your children may be shunned, isolated, and subject to physical violence from their peers. Individuals affected by HIV and AIDS are often denied health care and education. A recent report found that in one state in India, children from households in which someone had died of AIDS were often attacked or held in contempt by their classmates.[29] This can result in profound loneliness and depression for those living with and affected by HIV and AIDS. One Ethiopian woman told an interviewer: "Because I have the virus in my blood, I came to understand that my father does not see me equally as his other daughters. I became really sad. I felt inferior and that I am below any person."[30]

This stigma can have dangerous consequences. It can keep people from getting tested for HIV or from taking steps to protect themselves and others. This limits the number of people who can take advantage of programs to prevent the transmission of HIV from mothers to their unborn babies or gain access to antiretroviral therapy and other HIV and AIDS care services. The weight of this stigma can quickly lead to fatalism or cause an increase in destructive behavior, like indiscriminate sex and drug use, which increases the risk of transmitting HIV. Stigma within churches and faith communities can cause people to deny care for church and community members living with HIV and AIDS or for the orphans and vulnerable children whom they leave behind when they die.

Governmental and Societal Weakness

Countries with high infection rates are finding that it is threatening their ability to govern at every level; law enforcement, security, health care, education, and financial stability are all under attack. The AIDS pandemic is eroding the ability of several African governments

A recent report found that in one state in India, children from households in which someone had died of AIDS were often attacked or held in contempt by their classmates.

to provide social services and, as a result, has reduced their legitimacy. Governments dealing with economic collapse and institutional deterioration may be unable to fend off internal and external threats. These countries may be vulnerable to the kind of chaos and state collapse seen in Somalia and the Democratic Republic of the Congo (DRC).

> *African militaries have infection rates two to five times higher than their respective civilian populations, with extremely high military prevalence at rates as elevated as 60% for Angola and the DRC, 30% for Tanzania, and 20% for Cote d'Ivoire and Nigeria.*

AIDS can become a national security issue. African militaries have infection rates two to five times higher than their civilian populations, with military prevalence at rates as high as 60% for Angola and the DRC, 30% for Tanzania, and 20% for Cote d'Ivoire and Nigeria.[31] Furthermore, because of the long development period of the disease, AIDS is tearing into command structures because it kills soldiers after they have undergone considerable training and leadership development.[32] Domestic security is affected by the high infection rates within police forces and the judiciary system as well. AIDS accounted for 75% of all police deaths in Kenya in 1999 and 2000, and it is taking a similar toll on the police forces of many other nations.[33]

Financial Deterioration

For many countries, what began as a health care crisis has become a severe financial problem, threatening to further weaken struggling economies. A shrinking workforce and the rising costs of unhealthy employees affects both small and large businesses. This loss is quickly weakening national economies, and the additional costs of AIDS-related expenses—education and treatments—form a downward economic spiral that threatens not only businesses but also national budgets.

For private businesses, sickness and death from AIDS destroy human capital, boost absenteeism, and reduce the productivity of workers. HIV and AIDS hit hardest at Africa's most productive workers, with clusters found in middle and upper management and in the ranks of skilled workers.[34] When employees fall ill, the costs to businesses of absenteeism, retraining, and rising health benefit expenditures are steep. Several companies with operations in Africa, including giants such as Coca-Cola, Anglo-American Mining, and Botswana's Debswana Mines, have addressed the problem through education and antiretroviral programs.[35] Anecdotal evidence from South Africa suggests that a large number of firms are cutting employee pension and health benefits, and even engaging in unscrupulous AIDS-testing and dismissal practices.[36]

The burden on national budgets has been increasing as well. As more people are left without health benefits, government budgets have to absorb much of this burden, both in the rising costs of treatment for HIV, AIDS, and opportunistic infections, and in falling tax revenues from a shrinking corporate and individual tax base. In Botswana, the Institute for Development Policy Analysis predicts that AIDS-related expenditures will increase to 20% of the government budget by 2010, while the epidemic will cause overall government revenue to drop by 7%.[37] Falling productivity, lower corporate profits, declining tax revenues, and a rising fiscal burden all point to slower growth over the short run.

> In Botswana the Institute for Development Policy Analysis predicts that AIDS-related expenditures will increase to 20% of the government budget by 2010, while the epidemic will cause overall government revenue to drop by 7%.

The Gross Domestic Product (GDP)—a country's annual profits and income—of heavily affected countries is expected to fall by 0.3% to 1.5% per year.[38] A 2003 World Bank report predicted that even South Africa—which currently accounts for more than one-third of southern Africa's total GDP—will experience an economic collapse in less than three generations if nothing is done to reduce HIV infection rates and improve the education and care of orphans and vulnerable children.[39]

These declining numbers point to the potential for a fall in government expenditures across the African continent. When faced with falling tax revenues and rising fiscal costs, governments will be forced to cut spending on projects—such as road maintenance and telecommunications infrastructure—that are vital for future economic development and growth. In short, the AIDS pandemic will slow down the development of developing nations and even roll back approximately 20 years of progress.

breaking the cycles

After reading through this chapter, you may feel that the current state of affairs and the future look bleak. The intent is to give you the full picture of the AIDS pandemic, and all of the related factors, so that you can better understand the problem and possible solutions. There is hope ahead. The next two chapters focus on strategies for breaking the vicious cycles and provide practical steps that you can take on your own or with others to make these strategies a reality.

flowers for sale

On the way to the World Vision Women and AIDS Project office in Mumbai, India, there is a frail woman who sits at her doorstep and makes bouquets and garlands out of fresh flowers. Her three children—a 6-year-old son and daughters, 4 years and 6 months—sit around her. Lata works because her husband is HIV-positive and is in the hospital with tuberculosis. Lata is also infected, as is her oldest daughter. Her son is not infected, and her baby is still too young to get tested.

In an effort to help Lata, World Vision has sponsored her son and placed him in an English kindergarten, at Lata's request. World Vision also introduced her to the local church. The church leaders visit her regularly, and Lata has benefited greatly from spiritual counseling. Whenever Lata's daughter requires medical attention, World Vision takes her to a local doctor and pays her medical expenses. It is also is providing Lata with grants to help her continue her flower business.

Still, Lata's life is terribly difficult. Her 4-year-old girl looks like a 2-year-old. She has boils all over her body. As she sits outside with her mother, mosquitoes land on her arms and face. She does not have the strength to keep them away. On rare occasions she smiles, but seldom does she talk.

Lata is content if she is able to make enough money to buy provisions for the day. With the balance she buys fresh flowers for the next day's work, and small toys and candy to comfort her sick daughter, if there is anything left over. But the flower business is her only source of income, and it is only as consistent as Lata's health. She recently had to stop when she fell sick and could not buy milk for her baby for days on end.

discussion questions

Q The key takeaway from this chapter is that HIV does not exist in a vacuum by itself—it is being spread and contracted in countries that are already battling other societal problems. Some of the cycles described are cultural, some environmental, and most are the result of long-term poverty. Before we get to the next chapter, which discusses what is being done in the fight against AIDS, do you have any thoughts on how to address these issues? It's okay to start small.

Q Proverbs 29:7 says, "A righteous man knows the rights of the poor; a wicked man does not understand such knowledge" (ESV). How does this verse help you understand how to respond to this pandemic? How does this verse fit into the broader message of Scripture?

action items

1. Like Lindsay Schmidt, the graduate student described in the opening of this chapter, could you find a way to combine your current education or future career

with the fight against the AIDS pandemic? Think about potential ways your field might intersect with the global fight against AIDS. If there aren't clear ties between your future career and AIDS, are there ways the skills you're learning could be used in AIDS education or advocacy efforts?

2. Read James 1:27 and reread the section "Those Suffering in a Broken World." What should our response as Christians be to those most hurt by this crisis? Consider the victims' value in the eyes of God and their value in the broken societies of our world. How can we begin to show that we value the things of God in our response to the AIDS pandemic?

3. Look back through the chapter and pray for the victims most affected by the vicious cycles at work at every level of a society. Pray that God's kingdom would come in these countries and that the cycles would begin to reverse. Study verses about the kingdom of God in the Gospels for messages of hope in the face of suffering. Finally, prayerfully consider how God would have you care for His people who are suffering at the hands of this disease.

Chapter 3

Strategies for Restoration

getting people talking

Being surrounded by children affected by AIDS while he was volunteering at a center in his native country, Ethiopia, changed Wondriad's life forever. The children's pleas for help, and the stigma they faced, challenged him to do something. And he did.

Now at Pepperdine University, thousands of miles away from his home, Wondriad remembers those children. He recalls losing someone close to him and ponders the hundreds of people in his native land who are dying every day. No one at Pepperdine had been talking about AIDS. That was about to change. Wondriad had something to say, and his campus was about to be transformed forever.

"People need to hear about this. No one knows. No one is aware of this death here on campus. No one understands." Wondriad spurred his peers to join the Acting on AIDS movement. Together they engaged their campus on World AIDS Day through "Lives Are at Stake" (you can read more about this in chapter 4). Wondriad participated in the Acting on AIDS Student Leadership Summit, planned a successful AIDS awareness week on Pepperdine's campus, and widely shared his personal story. As a result, Wondriad and his campus community are more than willing to talk about this problem—they're ready to take an active stance on this issue.

"If your brother becomes poor and sells part of his property, then his nearest redeemer shall come and redeem what his brother has sold . . . . If your brother

becomes poor and cannot maintain himself with you, you shall support him as though he were a stranger and a sojourner, and he shall live with you. Take no interest from him or profit, but fear your God, that your brother may live beside you. . . . I am the LORD your God, who brought you out of the land of Egypt to give you the land of Canaan, and to be your God."
(Leviticus 25:25, 36, 38, ESV)

preventing the spread of HIV

As we've seen, the AIDS pandemic has been fueled by a diverse set of factors. Personal choices to engage in risky behavior drive the spread of HIV. As we discussed in the previous chapter, many factors and environments can limit people's ability to choose healthy behavior or may encourage them to pursue destructive paths. Factors such as wife inheritance and female genital

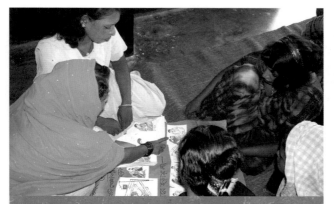

Through group discussions, posters, and pictures, peer-educators of World Vision's Mymensingh HIV Prevention Project in Bangladesh help build awareness among vulnerable groups, including brothel-based sex workers.

mutilation, gender inequalities, poverty, powerlessness, population mobility, drug use and trafficking, commercial sex, government instability, and social and economic decline, both drive the spread of HIV and AIDS and are worsened by its spread. This creates vicious cycles of HIV and AIDS vulnerability.

This complex environment demands a comprehensive and holistic approach that encourages positive choices and empowers individuals to overcome the barriers to making better choices.

The ABC Approach

Public health research states that the beginning of a broad approach to preventing the sexual transmission of HIV is the ABC approach, which stands for Abstinence, Being faithful to a spouse, and, in certain situations, using a Condom. World Vision is committed to doing all it can to honor both the sanctity of marriage and the sanctity of life (James 2:10–11). It promotes fidelity within marriage and abstinence outside of marriage as God's desired sexual behavior. At the same time, in situations where abstinence is not chosen, World Vision does not discourage the responsible use of condoms, because condoms have been demonstrated to reliably prevent the transmission of the deadly virus that causes AIDS. Because of the extremely tough choices that people in dire poverty may face, as discussed in the previous chapter, and the vulnerability of widows and orphans, condoms offer the opportunity to preserve lives.

> *Public health research states that the beginning of a broad approach to preventing the sexual transmission of HIV is the ABC approach, which stands for Abstinence, Being faithful to a spouse, and, in certain situations, using a Condom.*

The cornerstones of this approach, abstinence from sex before marriage and being faithful to a spouse, promote a scriptural view of sexuality, which protects people from the physical, emotional, and spiritual consequences of sex outside of marriage. Marriage is a holy gift from God that is designed to bless His children and give them opportunity for intimacy and long-lasting trust. It is a foundation for family and community, and it reflects the covenant relationship that God has with His church. The Bible gives us clear instruction to be faithful within marriage and abstinent outside of marriage. Promoting God's perfect

The children of sex workers attend a World Vision-supported preschool in the brothel village of Banishanta, home to 250 prostitutes. The school falls within the Mongla ADP area in Bangladesh and teaches 20 children.

ideal for people—through abstinence and faithfulness—will always be in their best interest.

The ABC approach has been a source of controversy due to strongly held beliefs by some groups that believe prevention should only emphasize either A or C. Groups that focus only on A believe that promoting condoms condones promiscuity by reducing the physical risk of this activity. Without such risk, they believe people would be unable or unwilling to control their passions. Groups that emphasize C believe that sexual behavior cannot be changed. They believe humans are controlled by their physical desires and a "realistic" program will focus on risk reduction under the assumption that people's sexual behavior will not change.

Results from Abstinence and Faithfulness

An emphasis on the A and B components of the ABC approach is the most reliable method for preventing the transmission of HIV, especially in areas of poverty, illiteracy, and instability.[1] There have been programs implemented by a number of governments—the most effective of which is in Uganda—that have focused on primary behavior change, or risk avoidance, with great success. Consistent messages encouraging changes in sexual behavior have had a significant impact in Uganda, Senegal, Jamaica, and the Dominican Republic.[2] In these countries, young people have delayed sexual intercourse until they were older and reduced the number of sexual partners they had once they became sexually active. This has reduced the spread of HIV.

Dr. Edward C. Green, a senior research scientist at Harvard University's Center for Population and Development Studies, writes in his book, *Rethinking AIDS Prevention,* about the decline in Ugandan HIV prevalence in the 1990s. He says, "Decline in infection rates is greatest among the 15 to 19 age group, and a UN-AIDS analysis shows that this was mostly due to the rise in the median age of first intercourse by 2 years, increasing from 15 to 17. Rise in age of sexual debut among females is particularly important because of the increased biological vulnerability of young females to HIV infection."

Consistent messages encouraging changes in sexual behavior have had a significant impact in Uganda, Senegal, Jamaica, and the Dominican Republic. In these countries, young people have delayed sexual intercourse until they were older and reduced the number of sexual partners they had once they became sexually active. This has reduced the spread of HIV.

Uganda's HIV prevention campaign, initiated by President Yoweri Museveni in 1986, focused primarily on abstinence and faithfulness messages until the mid 1990s, when condoms became more available and condom promotion was added as a key element of the program.[3] HIV and AIDS prevalence peaked and started to decline in 1991, three years before condoms were promoted in 1994.[4] HIV and AIDS prevalence declined from 20.6% in 1991 to 16% in 1994.[5]

According to Uganda's national HIV and AIDS prevalence data, HIV and AIDS prevalence declined from 20.6% in 1991 to 16% in 1994.

Dr. Green argues that this decline was due to substantial increases in abstinence and faithfulness before 1994, while condom use remained low. An adolescent fertility survey conducted between 1988 and 1990 found that, during the previous three years, "two thirds of the males had had more than one sexual partner; of these males, more than half had had four or more partners."[6] By 1995, the U.S. Agency for International Development Demographic and Health Survey for Uganda found that 95% of unmarried men and women ages 15 to 49 were reporting either one or zero casual sexual partners during the previous six months, with the vast majority of unmarried men and women (80.4% of men and 94.7% of women) reporting total abstinence. Among married people, 90.3% of men and 98.5% of women reported total fidelity to their spouses.[7]

During this period in Uganda, condom use was very rare. Five percent of rural Ugandan males, 18% of urban males, and less than 1% of rural and urban females reported using condoms between 1988 and 1990.[8] Also, a major Columbia/Johns Hopkins University study found that only 10% of men and 2% of women in their sample in Uganda reported consistent condom use in 1994.[9]

This data suggests that messages encouraging abstinence and faithfulness can lead to a substantial reduction in the transmission of HIV and a reduction in the number of people affected by AIDS.

Results from Condom Usage

Other countries that have implemented major condom promotion and access policies, without also focusing on abstinence and fidelity, have not found positive results.

South Africa and Zimbabwe have seen much higher rates of condom usage than Uganda. In 1999, Zimbabwe reported that 70% of men used condoms during their last high-risk sexual experience, and 28% used condoms during their last sexual encounter (with a spouse or non-regular partner). In 2002, South Africa reported that 30% of respondents reported condom use during their last sexual encounter. Their rates were much higher than in Uganda, which in 2000–2001 reported 59% condom use during high-risk sex and 15% during the last sexual encounter. It might seem that HIV prevalence would have declined significantly in both South Africa and Zimbabwe as a result of these statistics. Yet prevalence rates in

Data from Thailand shows that condom promotion among high-risk groups was very successful in controlling an anticipated AIDS epidemic among commercial sex participants.

Zimbabwe and South Africa in 2003 were 24.6% and 21.5%, respectively, both up slightly from 2001.[10] Ugandan prevalence is 6.7% in 2006,[11] down from 20.6% in 1991.[12]

However, data from Thailand shows that condom promotion among high-risk groups was very successful in controlling an anticipated AIDS epidemic among commercial sex participants. Thailand instilled a policy of mandatory condom use for all commercial sex, which helped to prevent the spread of HIV among sex workers and patrons. The policy did not bring down prevalence rates elsewhere in the region, suggesting that condom promotion works best when promoted along with abstinence and being faithful. Dr. Green stated in a recent interview that: "[A and B] was part of Thailand's programs that most people don't know about. There was a campaign to get men to not go to prostitutes, to not have multiple partners, for young males not to have sex at an early age. And it worked. In the early years of the 1990s, the proportion of men reporting pre-marital and extra-marital sex and going to brothels went down significantly."[13]

In populations outside of high-risk groups (sex workers and clients), consistent condom use is as low as 5%. When condoms are not used with 100% consistency, the effectiveness drops to 0%.

While consistent condom use can be 80 to 90% effective in preventing the spread of HIV and other sexually transmitted diseases, consistent condom use is rare. In populations outside of high-risk groups (sex workers and clients), consistent condom use is as low as 5%. When condoms are not used with 100% consistency, the effectiveness drops to 0%.[14]

Blood-to-Blood Transmission

In the effort to help prevent the spread of AIDS through blood-to-blood transmission, there are two main approaches: risk avoidance and risk reduction. Risk avoidance efforts focus on avoiding the possibility of becoming infected, mostly through programs that prevent new drug addictions and offer treatment and counseling programs for people who are already addicted. Risk reduction efforts focus on reducing the risk of infection for those who continue to use drugs, through education and providing clean needles and syringes. This section will discuss the efforts of both approaches.

Combating Drug Addiction

The primary group at risk for acquiring HIV through blood-to-blood transmission is drug users. AIDS is transmitted through the sharing of needles, syringes, and other drug paraphernalia. The best way for this group to avoid the risk of infection is to stop injecting drugs, possibly through programs that offer treatment and counseling to drug addicts. Some programs help intravenous drug users switch to smoking, snorting, or other methods that don't involve injecting.

Intravenous drugs, such as heroin and cocaine, are illegal throughout the world, and many countries are wrestling with the trade-off between punishing people who break the law and encouraging people to seek help for their addictions.

The reality of promoting risk avoidance in the context of drug use is complicated. Intravenous drugs, such as heroin and cocaine, are illegal throughout the world, and many countries are wrestling with the trade-off between punishing people who break the law and encouraging people to seek help for their addictions. In addition, there is a great deal of controversy about the best way to treat people who are addicted to heroin. In Russia, a country with almost 3 million drug users, methadone is illegal. Methadone is a common medical substitute for heroin that is used in replacement therapy.[15]

Combating addiction is a key factor to removing roadblocks to healthy choices. In many developing countries, those involved in drug use are also often involved in sex work as a way to pay for their habit. Heavy drug and alcohol users are much more likely to engage in casual sex when under the influence. Treating addiction helps break this cycle of destructive behavior. One study found that, among heterosexual alcoholics one year into recovery, there was a 58% drop in intravenous drug use as well as large decreases in high-risk sexual behaviors.[16]

One study found that, among heterosexual alcoholics one year into recovery, there was a 58% drop in intravenous drug use as well as large decreases in high-risk sexual behaviors.

Freeing people from addiction is consistent with our charge as Christians to free prisoners from their chains. Addiction is both a physical illness and a spiritual captivity. Jesus came to heal the sick and to set the captives free (Luke 4:18). This release from bondage and oppression, and the healing of sickness and blindness, were prophesied in Isaiah 61 as characteristics of the Messiah. This is the hope that World Vision and the members of Acting on AIDS aspire to extend to others.

NEP and SEP Approaches

Perhaps the most controversial approach for those who promote risk reduction is the use of needle exchange programs (NEP) and syringe exchange programs (SEP). NEP have been shown to be important elements in preventing the spread of HIV among intravenous drug users, but only if they are part of a more comprehensive prevention program. Several studies have also concluded that needle exchange programs do not have a negative effect on the society around them, a major fear of those opposed to risk reduction strategies. NEP have been shown not to increase the rate of injection among drug users,[17] not to promote drug use among adolescents,[18] not to increase the number of discarded needles in adjacent geographic areas, and not to lead to connections between different injecting networks.[19]

NEP have been shown not to increase the rate of injection among drug users, not to promote drug use among adolescents, not to increase the number of discarded needles in adjacent geographic areas, and not to lead to connections between different injecting networks.

However, NEP and SEP have also not been conclusively shown to decrease the risk of injecting drug users becoming HIV-positive. In many contexts, NEP and SEP often do not offer sterile paraphernalia, includ-

> *Many NEP and SEP do not integrate sexual risk prevention into their programs, which is a major problem because drug use is highly associated with risky sexual behavior.*

ing the cotton swabs used to filter the drug solution, the rinse cups used to wash out syringes, and the "cooker" used to prepare the solution.[20] Another problem is that many NEP and SEP do not integrate sexual risk prevention into their programs, which is a major problem because drug use is highly associated with risky sexual behavior. Also, many needle and syringe exchange programs do not offer a holistic program that includes treatment and counseling for addiction. Helping individuals to recover from addiction is the best way to prevent the sharing of needles.

removing roadblocks to choice

The vicious cycles described in chapter 2—poverty, gender inequality, drug trafficking, migration, poor education, food scarcity, and others—that limit choice or encourage harmful choices seem hopeless due to their scale and the depth of their roots. But they are not intractable. Hope lies in empowering people by removing roadblocks to choice, then trusting in God's power to multiply these efforts by the creation of *virtuous cycles* that can combat the effects of the vicious cycles currently at work. The following examples—microenterprise and improving education—are just two of the myriad of ways that roadblocks can be removed.

Economic Opportunities through Microenterprise

Because HIV and AIDS are prevalent in regions associated with poverty, improving socioeconomic prospects in these regions has a significant positive impact. Microenterprise development (MED) has been shown to help improve people's lives both socially and economically. MED is the process of providing training and credit to people who do not have access to a formal credit system, such as bank loans. MED programs provide block loans to a group of borrowers, who then divide the loan among individuals who repay the loan as a group. All members are held jointly accountable to repay the entire loan amount. Loans are for small amounts, often around US$150 per person in African countries, and usually come due in less than one year. After repaying a loan, the group of borrowers are eligible to apply for another loan and can continue to build their businesses. Repayment rates are very high—often over 95%.[21]

Microenterprise development can help provide economic opportunities within communities, enabling both men and women to avoid dangerous work and empowering women to negotiate respect and better roles within their community.

Microenterprise development can help provide economic opportunities within communities, enabling both men and women to avoid dangerous work and empowering women to negotiate respect and better roles within their community. MED can also help provide a safety net—through increased savings, basic insurance, and access to credit—

Josephine, 16, earns enough money repairing clothes to buy cassava flour, the cheapest food available. Josephine supports her younger sister, her older, sick brother, and his wife. They live in Muyinga province, Burundi, and were orphaned by AIDS six years ago.

which can enable families affected by AIDS to avoid selling productive assets, such as land and tools, to buy food and to pay for medical and funeral expenses. MED training has also been shown to be an excellent forum for conveying information and having community conversations about HIV and AIDS.[22]

World Vision has a program that seeks to improve the lives of very poor women in rural East Africa by combining economic development assistance with improved access to HIV and AIDS care, mitigation services, and education. The program is called PRISMA and stands for Promote Rural Integration and Security through Microfinance in Africa. Women are a primary focus because they tend to invest the additional income they earn improving the lives of their children. For example, studies show that poor women entrepreneurs use 92 cents of each dollar of extra income to improve their children's health and education.[23]

> Studies show that poor women entrepreneurs use 92 cents of each dollar of extra income to improve their children's health and education.

When women are empowered to earn an income, they not only gain financial clout, their husbands also have opportunities to remain closer to home, rather than seeking work through migration, which may lead to other sexual relationships. As women experience financial independence, their sense of empowerment grows, and family and community relationships are changed. When women no longer are constrained by economic forces, they can choose not to participate in sexual relationships that are dangerous and degrading. When they can repay business loans they become financially stable and better equipped to negotiate their roles within the community. This personal transformation can lead to social transformation, establishing the necessary seedbed for HIV prevention.

Improving Education

Increasing access to education also is an important aspect of HIV prevention, particularly for girls and orphans. The World Bank states that "education may be the single most effective preventive weapon against HIV/AIDS."[24]

> *Even completing primary school can greatly reduce a child's vulnerability to becoming HIV-positive.*

Children who attend kindergarten through grade 12 are more likely to learn how to protect themselves from contracting HIV. Yet, in many poor families, providing school fees, uniforms, and supplies can be a major barrier that prevents children from attending school, especially for girls and orphans. As previously discussed, in many developing nations boys are often sent to school before girls, since boys are assumed to have better opportunities to use their education to earn an income to support the family. However, when girls or boys complete secondary school, their employment and economic opportunities increase. This decreases their susceptibility to HIV infection. Even completing primary school can greatly reduce a child's vulnerability to becoming HIV-positive. Approximately 700,000 cases of HIV in young adults could be prevented each year—7 million in a decade.[25]

In 2000 the World Bank relaunched a 1990 initiative called "Education for All."[26] This program aims to provide universal primary education, thus achieving the second of the United Nation's Millennium Development Goals.[27] This program will direct donor funds to ensure all children have access to primary education worldwide by 2015. This achievement will substantially increase adult literacy, narrow the literacy gap between

Children attending a Nyarurama primary school Anti-HIV and AIDS Club in Rwanda perform a traditional dance during the competitions.

men and women, and eliminate gender disparities in primary and secondary education. Part of the annual savings from the $56 billion Multilateral Debt Relief Initiative (MDRI), which was enacted by a group of eight major industrial countries in 2005, is earmarked for achieving these goals.[28] The MDRI is part of the Heavily Indebted Poor Countries (HIPC) program—an initiative of the International Monetary Fund and World Bank—initially aimed to help poor countries manage their debt loads through economic reform, debt relief, and rescheduling.[29] The MDRI initiative provides 100% debt relief for all HIPC countries that complete the HIPC program or have a per capita income below $380 per person and are heavily indebted. As of May 1, 2006, 20 countries had reached this point.[30] Tanzania, one of the initial countries to graduate from the HIPC program, has significantly increased education spending and eliminated school fees for primary education. This has helped roughly 1.6 million children go back to school.[31]

care for adults and children affected by HIV and AIDS

Even if heavily infected countries substantially reduce new HIV infections, there are still 40 million people in the world living with HIV. AIDS has orphaned more than 15 million children under the age of 18, and 12 million of them live in sub-Saharan Africa.[32] An additional 12 million children in sub-Saharan Africa are estimated to be vulnerable from AIDS.[33] "Vulnerable" means the children who are living with chronically ill parents, children living in households fostering orphans, or any other children who meet the definition of extreme poverty in their communities. By 2010, it is estimated that more than one out of every five children in sub-Saharan Africa will either be orphaned or vulnerable due to AIDS and other causes.[34] Breaking the vicious cycle means providing care for adults living with HIV and AIDS in order to prolong their lives as providers, parents, and positive members of their communities. It also requires nurturing and educating orphans and vulnerable children so that they can grow up to take their parents' places as productive members of society.

BY 2010, it is estimated that more than one out of every five children in Africa will either be orphaned or vulnerable due to AIDS.

People Living with HIV and AIDS

It is crucial to provide people living with HIV and AIDS access to a continuum of care. This continuum includes training on how to "live positively." This training gives people information on nutrition, health, exercise, sleep, and other vital personal care elements. It also includes basic home-based care; the provision of antiretroviral therapy (ART) to keep the virus from replicating; and provides information on how to manage opportunistic infections like thrush, diarrhea, and other digestive problems typical for people living with HIV and AIDS.

Access to ART can dramatically improve the quality of an infected person's life. Studies from Brazil, South Africa, Haiti, India, and other developing countries show that ART helps people living with AIDS gain weight, fight opportunistic infections, reduce the levels of HIV in their blood, and live longer and healthier lives.[35] ART has major benefits for families,

A 29-year-old woman in the last stages of AIDS. Mrs. Indira Muthu Mudaliar is sick with tuberculosis and is bedridden 50% of the time. She participates in an HIV and AIDS care project in India.

health systems, and societies. First, parents gain many more years to nurture their children and equip them for adult life. Second, broad-based ART programs may result in substantial cost savings for health systems when all costs are taken into account.[36] Initial research suggests that properly managed ART programs may improve health staff morale because overall health systems and results are improved. ART programs benefit people who suffer from other diseases and who are often crowded out of the hospital system by HIV and AIDS patients.[37] Third, ART programs may reduce stigma and increase voluntary counseling and testing. This life-saving treatment gives people the hope they need to get tested for HIV and to begin telling their friends and family about their illness. With ART, HIV stops being a death sentence, something to hide from and deny, and starts being a reality people can manage and for which they receive support.

> *With ART, HIV stops being a death sentence, something to hide from and deny, and starts being a reality people can manage and for which they receive support.*

Even without ART, there are other tactics that can help people living with HIV and AIDS live longer and better lives. Encouraging churches and other faith communities to talk about HIV in a loving and supportive way helps to reduce the stigma that surrounds HIV and gives people confidence to get tested. Counseling for depression and other psychological disorders associated with HIV helps people living with HIV and AIDS work through their feelings of trauma, grief, and loss. Mobilizing volunteers to provide home-based care can improve the patient's quality of life; volunteers can clean clothes and bedding, apply ointments to sooth skin sores, give pain relievers, and help with household chores. Home-based care also takes the burden off of the patient's children—enabling them to go to school and prepare for their futures.

> *Encouraging churches and other faith communities to talk about HIV in a loving and supportive way helps to reduce the stigma that surrounds HIV and gives people confidence to get tested.*

Caring for OVC

Care and support of orphans and vulnerable children (OVC) is crucial for preventing the cycles of disease and poverty from being transmitted across generations. However, the predominant, historic strategy of caring for OVC in orphanages and similar institutions is an extremely expensive solution and cannot hope to support the millions of children who need care.[38] Also, institutional care has been shown to be undesirable in the long run because it takes children out of their communities and robs them of social connections and the chance to develop long-term relationships.[39]

For these reasons, World Vision, and many of the largest donor organizations and child-focused agencies in the world—the U.S., British, and Danish governments, U.N. agencies, Save the Children, CARE, and others—have identified community-based care as the best strategy for caring for orphans and vulnerable children.[40]

World Vision offers a program called Community Care Coalitions (CCC). Through the CCC model, World Vision gathers a group of concerned community members who are already taking responsibility for assisting OVC or other vulnerable community members, or who are interested in doing so. These community members often come from churches, other faith communities, community-based organizations, local businesses, government, and other local institutions.

> The predominant, historic strategy of caring for OVC in orphanages and similar institutions is an extremely expensive solution and cannot hope to support the millions of children who need care.

These coalitions work with World Vision to identify the most vulnerable children in their communities and then recruit "home visitors," or community volunteers who commit to visiting OVC regularly. These home visitors are trained by World Vision to monitor the well-being of the children, protect them against abuse and neglect, provide psychosocial support and basic counseling, help them learn life skills, advocate for their rights at the local level, and assist them with any other needs that may arise. When possible, World Vision also helps to support the volunteer caregivers by facilitating support groups and providing follow-up training.

> While institutional care often costs well over $1,000 per child per year, community-based care that provides a caring home visitor and some material support can cost significantly less. World Vision's programs in several African countries cost several times less.

In addition, CCC work to overcome barriers to education, give referrals to health-care workers, help with chores, provide home-based care for sick parents, train OVC in proper nutrition and hygiene, help them to plan for the deaths of their parents (if parents are still alive), and provide food and clothing when it is available.

Through the mobilization and support of CCC, and other programs that leverage the talent and passion already contained within communities, the international community can care for millions of orphans and vulnerable children. While institutional care often costs well over $1,000 per child per year,[41] community-based care that provides a caring home visitor and some material support can cost significantly less. World Vision's programs in Kenya, Uganda, Zambia, and Mozambique on average cost several times less than the cost of institutional care.[42] Mobilizing community-based care—by providing training and mentoring programs for caregivers—also has the advantage of increasing the skills and capacity of community members. The use of passionate volunteers can increase the sustainability of these interventions far beyond the life of any one program.

This approach in caring for orphans and vulnerable children decreases the risk that they will become HIV-positive and increases the hope that the negative cycle of vulnerability will be broken.

conclusion

This chapter presented some of the efforts that have been effective in breaking the cycle of AIDS and poverty. The next chapter will give you some tools for how to inspire and mobilize your community to make a difference for people affected by HIV and AIDS around the world.

Madalina

Madalina is 11. She lives with her parents and her younger sister in Lazu, a small village near Constantia, Romania. Madalina was a healthy girl at birth, but when she was 4 months old, Madalina came down with a lung infection. Doctors gave her blood transfusions to combat the infection, which contained HIV-infected blood.

In 1995, when Madalina was diagnosed with HIV, her mother, Cristina, accepted the diagnosis and started to fight for her daughter's health. She never treated Madalina as a sick child and offered her everything she could, though the family had little money.

Her family does not have anything but their hands and 5 acres of land. World Vision helps them to use their resources well. Cristina would like to organize a small farm with a neighbor who also is caring for an HIV-positive daughter. Cristina says that God brought World Vision into her family, and she is sure that the organization will help Madalina have a normal and happy life.

discussion questions

Q Wondriad, the student in the introduction to this chapter, was most concerned with the stigma and silence that accompanies AIDS in his home country of Ethiopia. Do you feel there is a stigma against AIDS in your country or community? How would an HIV-positive person be treated at your school or in your church? Why do you think this is, and how do you think you should respond?

Q Read Genesis 38:13–19, 24–26. Tamar was included in the lineage of Jesus, yet she made a very controversial decision in an effort to survive. Stories like Tamar's deserve study when considering the choices people make in the face of poverty. What does this story show us about God's heart for people who are faced with these kinds of decisions?

Q Some of the efforts to prevent the sexual transmission of HIV described in this chapter have some controversy behind them, like using just the A and B or just the C approach. Occasionally the argument is offered that there is not a method that would be successful for all people groups or all faith backgrounds. If you had to choose between A and B or C for your loved ones, which method would you use? If you had sons or daughters attending university where population was 30–50% HIV-positive, would you encourage them toward the C method—considering the statistics—or toward the A and B method?

action items

1. December 1 is World AIDS Day. Do you know what events or programs are happening on your campus or in your community to raise awareness on this day? Find out if there are ways that you can get involved in what is already going on. If nothing is planned, perhaps this is an opportunity for you to get involved and start something. Please see the Acting on AIDS Web site for activities that will be held nationwide (www.worldvision.org/actingonaids).

2. Like Wondriad, are there ways you can help break the silence about AIDS on your campus? Brainstorm ways in which you can help end the stigma for people suffering from AIDS, both on a local and on a global scale.

3. Most importantly, keep praying. Pray that the efforts described in this chapter—the ABC approach, risk avoidance and reduction with respect to intravenous drug use, microenterprise development, "Education for All," ARTs, and Community Care Coalitions—would be blessed and would make an impact in preventing the spread and transmission of HIV. Ask that God would bless these programs with the funding and support that they need to be successful. And pray that the people who receive help through these efforts would see Jesus' love and redemption for them through the love and care of others.

4. When your faith motivates your actions, it will often open up doors to share your faith in words as well. Practice how you would do this. As you think about sharing your faith, look for verses in the Bible that explain why caring and advocating for those affected by HIV and AIDS is important.

Chapter 4

Create a Movement

make some noise

When 12 students at Anderson University in Indiana learned about the devastation AIDS was creating around the world, they knew they had to do something. Their advisor encouraged them that because this was the largest humanitarian crisis of our time, there was nothing they could do that would be too big or too outlandish in order to raise awareness. These students realized that their campus had been silent for far too long, so they started by making some noise.

Student leaders rang the campus bell every 14 seconds for six hours. Each bell represented another child who had been orphaned by AIDS. Students would have continued to ring the bell had the university's administration not asked them to stop. But by the end of the day, they had made their point, and they did it creatively. Their noise started a movement. Overnight, more than 150 students joined their cause. A revival began on their campus, which opened students' hearts to all sorts of global injustices, including AIDS.

> "Then the King will say to those on his right, 'Come, you who are blessed by my Father; take your inheritance, the kingdom prepared for you since the creation of the world. For I was hungry and you gave me something to eat, I was thirsty and you gave me something to drink, I was a stranger and you invited me in, I needed clothes and you clothed me, I was sick and you looked after me, I was in prison and you came to visit me.'" (Matthew 25:34–36, NIV)

Chapter leaders at Anderson University ring a bell every 14 seconds. Each ring represents another child who is orphaned by HIV/AIDS.

This generation is constantly inundated with messages, pitches, and promotions. It is probably the most marketed-to generation in the history of the world. Marketers realize that by investing in this generation, they are investing in the future of their products. Political parties understand that by appealing to the younger generations and by shaping its opinions, they can create lifetime voters. An investment in this generation is an investment in the future. In other words, your voice counts. People care about what you have to say and what you think.

What if rather than following the directions of others you began leading a new course? What if you use your voice and fight to end the vicious cycle of HIV and AIDS; to end the injustices of oppression; and to end the crippling impact of poverty around the world?

The global AIDS pandemic may seem hopeless, and you may often feel that there is nothing you can do. But even without the resources to send to a village in need or the expertise to empower a community around the world, you do have a voice that others will listen to. Perhaps the greatest impact this generation of Christians can have is making noise, raising awareness, and moving others to action: you can motivate your parents, friends, elected officials, local media, and corporations to respond to the AIDS pandemic and other issues of injustice.

Making noise takes creativity. Adding your voice to the mix of messages your peers receive by drilling them with statistics and cold facts may not communicate the devastation of AIDS to anyone.

Making noise takes creativity. Adding your voice to the mix of messages your peers receive by drilling them with statistics and cold facts may not communicate the devastation of AIDS to anyone. So be smarter and more strategic about how you communicate. Campaigns like "Do You See Orange?" illustrate the statistics and let people feel the impact that AIDS is having on children. The bell at Anderson University lets people hear just how many children are orphaned by AIDS every minute. If you want to make an impact in spreading the word about AIDS, you need to get creative.

create a movement

To create a movement, it is important to cast a vision. The vision for Acting on AIDS is to create awareness and activism on behalf of the global AIDS pandemic at colleges and universities across the nation. This vision was based on knowledge of the need caused by AIDS, prayer for God's will, and the resolve to take action through faith.

The vision for Acting on AIDS is to create awareness and activism on behalf of the global AIDS pandemic at colleges and universities across the nation.

By furthering your knowledge about this issue, you have taken the first step toward starting a movement. The next step is to pray for God to share his vision for the widowed, orphaned, and distressed. Then, you must resolve to respond by putting your faith into action. This part of the vision involves not just responding individually but getting others to act on behalf of those victimized by this pandemic.

Prayer

In the fall of 2005, thirty-five Christian college campuses wanted to find a way to combine efforts for World AIDS Day on December 1. Many students were already involved in fundraising and political advocacy campaigns on their campuses, but they wanted to introduce an activity in which every student could participate. They decided to come together in prayer.

A photo from the World AIDS Day activity, "Lives Are at Stake." Hundreds of stakes are placed on a central part of campus where students and faculty are encouraged to pull a stake out of the ground, wear a photo of a child impacted by HIV/AIDS and pray for that specific child and for the issue.

This effort was called "Lives Are at Stake," and its main objective was to encourage students to pray. Students were asked to pray for the millions of children around the world who have been orphaned or made vulnerable because of the impact AIDS is having on them, their communities, and their families. To make their message heard, on World AIDS Day students scattered hundreds of pictures and stories of children across their campuses. Some colleges placed the pictures on metal stakes; others hung them from doorknobs and handrails. Students, faculty, and surrounding community members were encouraged to take a picture of a child, read his or her story on the back, and pray for that child throughout the day. Everyone can pray; it is one of the most powerful ways in which you can take action against AIDS.

> *Everyone can pray; it is one of the most powerful ways in which you can take action against AIDS.*

In addition to encouraging others to pray, you need to consider developing a rich and vibrant personal prayer life. You can do this on your own or with others, but it is important to develop the discipline of consistent prayer.

Discipleship

Mother Teresa, who worked with the most destitute on the streets of Calcutta, including many AIDS victims, said that she did what she did because she always saw Jesus' face in the face of the poor. Discipleship is the journey of serving God and loving your neighbor in response to God's love for you.

> Discipleship is the journey of serving God and loving your neighbor in response to God's love for you.

Going deeper in your walk of faith is critical when getting involved in an issue that has wrought as much devastation as AIDS. If people don't have a good understanding of God and His character, if they don't have a proper perspective of Him as a good and just God, they can easily become overwhelmed by the size and scope of the AIDS pandemic and the lack of resources to address it. This can cause people to quickly become discouraged—not just in the fight against AIDS but in their faith as well. This is why it is imperative for you to get plugged into a Christian community that will encourage your discipleship. Consider learning more through your church or a campus ministry, a Bible study, or a small group. If you are going to make an impact in the fight against AIDS, you need to learn what it means to be a disciple of Christ.

The Bible is the ultimate resource for learning how to treat the sick and the poor. It shows us God's heart for this group of people and his vision for how the church should respond to them. This was a large focus of Jesus' ministry. In fact, half of the miracles that Jesus performs in the gospel of Luke are healing the sick. In his call to make disciples of all men, Jesus asks for relationship, for healing, and for spreading hope and good news. The book of James gives us more clarity about the importance of caring for others in our faith: "Religion that God our Father accepts as pure and faultless is this: to look after orphans and widows in their distress and to keep oneself from being polluted by the world" (James 1:27, NIV).

Half of the miracles that Jesus performs in the gospel of Luke are healing the sick.

Part of becoming a disciple of Christ involves joining God's effort to establish his kingdom on earth. This involves treating those that the world devalues—the powerless, the sick, women, orphans, and the poor—the way God sees them. All of us will face neediness, illness, and death in some form in our lifetime, but it is unjust for some to face it constantly. All of us have been given the opportunity for dignity and life through receiving the mercy of Christ, and we can extend it to others by sharing both his message and his love. Proverbs 19:17 says, "Whoever is generous to the poor lends to the LORD, and he will repay him for his deed" (ESV). In loving others we enter into the love that was given freely to us and enrich the kingdom of God.

the importance of advocacy

Advocating is simply speaking for others whose voices are not heard. The role of Acting on AIDS is to help students become advocates, and then train others to do the same. We do this out of a response to God's love, and by taking small, practical steps to raise awareness on behalf of others.

Faith and Advocacy

Advocacy can be a strategic and significant way to create positive change. All Christians are all called to be advocates. Your citizenship in God's kingdom is shown through the fruits, or outward response, of this membership. As an American, you need to understand the importance and the value of leveraging your citizenship. You must invest your citizenship—both spiritually and politically—by calling on God, the church, and this nation to care for those who are hurting, in need, or isolated.

Advocacy Is a Privilege and a Responsibility

Advocating government on behalf of those most affected by AIDS is a responsibility that requires you to be educated about the issue so that you know who to contact and what to advocate for. Those committed to this cause must encourage your nation's leaders to adopt policies and adequately fund programs that both respond to immediate health care needs and address the structural issues that keep people living in dire straits around the world. Governments worldwide can play a major role in resolving social inequalities that lead to desperate poverty, and you can leverage your privilege as an American citizen to encourage this role.

> You must invest your citizenship—both spiritually and politically—by calling on God, the church, and this nation to care for those who are hurting, in need, or isolated.

Encouraging government leaders and holding them accountable to care for the needs of the vulnerable and marginalized is a theme throughout Scripture. Working for just government action by supporting positive legislation in a bipartisan, balanced way allows Christians to speak out across party lines and faith traditions, and has proven to be effective in improving policies enacted in Washington. Requesting government action can result in lasting structural changes that may be caused by unjust policies.

Advocacy Requires Community

If one voice can make a difference, many voices joined together can create meaningful change in the lives of people living with HIV and AIDS. It is essential to work in community if we are going to make a difference in the fight against HIV and AIDS. This is why we encourage you to work with or start a chapter of Acting on AIDS or some other coalition. Strength comes in numbers when you are advocating. It's the only way you can make an impact at the governmental level.

> Strength comes in numbers when you are advocating. It's the only way you can make an impact at the governmental level.

Successful coalitions harness the diversity of their members, such as political and personal backgrounds, advocacy experience, skills, and locations. One of the greatest advantages to working as a community is that you increase the possibility that someone in your group—a college president or a business executive—will have relationships with local politicians. An influential member of the community can speak to a government representative on behalf of many people and help to make the issue personal to the elected official.

tools of advocacy

The prospect of contacting elected officials may be intimidating. But experienced advocates will tell you that it gets easier with practice. Fortunately, there are many ways that you can communicate with your representatives. Choose the one with whom you feel most comfortable, and know that even the shortest letter from a constituent speaks volumes to an elected official. Most elected officials keep careful track of how many letters, e-mails, and calls they receive on an issue as a way of gauging constituents' opinions. The fact that most constituents do not take the time to communicate with them means that when you do, it can represent many voices. As one person you can speak for many who feel the same way but do not write and, in the process, promote positive change.

> As one person you can speak for many who feel the same way but do not write and, in the process, promote positive change.

Using the influence of your citizenship can be done in creative, simple, and effective ways. The following are some tools you can use as you start on the road toward advocacy.

Writing Letters

What many people do not realize is that writing a letter to your political representative can actually make a difference. Congressional staff members say that all it takes is up to 20 handwritten letters to bring attention to an issue in a congressional office.[1] This makes letter writing a great tool for students since it takes a short amount of time and costs a few cents. You can have letter-writing gatherings at group meetings or after class. National, state, and local organizations such as Acting on AIDS can provide helpful information like sample letters and fact sheets. If you've been given a sample letter, personalize it by adding information about how the issue affects you, your community, or your program.

In general, an effective letter is only one page long. Address one issue and name one desired response per letter. This way your representative's staff will be able to compile your letter with similar letters in order to tally how many people share your same position. Be brief, courteous, and specific. Start and end your letter by stating why you are writing and what you are asking your representative to do. The tone of your letter should be polite, even if you disagree with a member's position or are expressing disappointment about an action they took.

Always address your legislator properly, making sure you've spelled his or her name correctly and have the right title. (For example, Senator Dianne Feinstein or Vice Admiral Richard H. Carmona, M.D., M.P.H., FACS. State senators should be addressed as Therese Murray, Massachusetts state senator; Massachusetts State Senator Therese Murray; or the Honorable Therese Murray; state representatives follow this same pattern.) Before you address your representative, look him or her up online to make sure you have everything correct.

Congressional staff members say that all it takes is up to 20 handwritten letters to bring attention to an issue in a congressional office.

For more targeted letters, write to representatives on key committees. Web sites—including the ones listed near the end of this chapter—and congressional guides in public libraries provide lists of the different congressional committees and what issues these committees address, as well as which members of Congress are involved.

If your elected official is not supportive of your request, find out why and see if you can address his or her concerns. If your representative responds, write a thank you note. It shows you care enough to watch how your representative responds. Be sure to track the progress of your issue in Congress, and let your representative know you voted on Election Day.

A few other things to keep in mind: Do not write to a representative who does not represent your area—many congressional offices disregard mail that is not from a constituent in their district or state. Faxing letters following these guidelines is one of the most effective tactics. Prior to the anthrax scare on Capitol Hill in the aftermath of 9/11, letters were the preferred method of communication for constituents, but today faxing is more readily received.

> *Do not write to a representative who does not represent your area—many congressional offices disregard mail that is not from a constituent in their district or state.*

Making Phone Calls

Sometimes legislation moves so quickly on Capitol Hill that there is no time to write letters; in that case, telephone calls are a fast and personal way to express your concerns. Calling your legislator is very effective, particularly in the days leading up to an important vote. To prepare for the phone conversation, jot down a few notes containing the key points you want to make, and refer to the notes during your call. Keep your message brief; it is important to request a specific and measurable action.

Unless you know your elected official personally, you will speak to someone on his or her staff. In fact, you may want to ask to speak with the legislative aide who handles health or HIV and AIDS issues. If an aide is not available, leave a message with the receptionist containing your name, address, and phone number. If you are with a group and will be generating numerous calls, ask other callers to also leave a message with the receptionist. Since you are trying to establish a positive relationship with the staff, you don't want to overload the legislative aide with too many calls. A few callers can contact the aide to let him or her know there are other messages with the receptionist.

Setting up a Phone Tree

To generate a persuasive number of calls, form a telephone-tree network of activists. Ask every person in the network to deliver a message to the congressional office. This flood of calls can sway an undecided vote or convince a legislator who wonders where the public stands on a particular issue. Here are a few steps to help you organize a phone tree:

To prepare for the phone conversation, jot down a few notes containing the key points you want to make, and refer to the notes during your call.

1. Make a list of the current phone numbers of everyone in your telephone tree.

2. Choose a coordinator and several key people. Think of the coordinator as the tree's trunk and the key people as the main branches. The coordinator will construct and pass along a message to the key people, who will be responsible for calling up to 10 people. The coordinator will also maintain the phone tree to make sure it stays current.

3. Give the key people the names and phone numbers of the people in the network they are responsible to call, as well as the name and phone number of the elected official being contacted.

4. Have the coordinator start the tree by passing along a short and concise message to the key people. Since the message will go through the tree, it needs to be clear enough for everyone to write down and repeat to the elected official.

5. Have the key people contact their list of callers to begin the tree. Once the callers make their calls, have them contact their key person to verify that the message went through.

6. Once the key people have heard confirmation from their callers, they should contact the coordinator so the coordinator knows the phone tree was successful.[2]

Here are more tools you can use to mobilize your community or campus chapter to advocate for AIDS issues:

- *Register to vote.* Voting should the first way you choose to leverage your citizenship. Use your vote to support candidates who care about the poor and marginalized and who will support policies that affect women and children who are vulnerable to AIDS.

- *Use lobby days.* Use days like World AIDS Day to organize students from a constituency, along with administrators from your college, to visit your congressional representative. Bring specific actions that this representative can take regarding legislation that would help those affected by AIDS. Remember to be respectful and offer measurable examples of success. The idea is to show that you are hopeful that this representative can make a difference and explain how this issue affects you as a voter. Make sure you are registered to vote and active in elections before you take this step.

- *Host campus forums and speakers.* Hold events to mobilize students on your campus by inviting speakers who are experts on HIV and AIDS to educate and encourage your campus into action. Acting on AIDS and World Vision have several speakers who can speak on many of the issues pertinent to AIDS and addressed in this book. Contact Acting on AIDS at actingonaids@worldvision.org or (253) 815-1000 for more information. These speaking events can also help to mobilize your Acting on AIDS chapter and interested members of the community. Invite local politicians and members of the media to maximize the opportunity to raise awareness and encourage others toward action.

- *Send e-mail alerts.* E-mail allows you to distribute detailed information, instructions, and sample letters to Congress to large lists of individuals in an inexpensive and convenient way. The ability to forward an e-mail helps engage others who may not be involved directly in the issue but who would be willing to take action, if asked.

- *Utilize postcards.* From time to time, World Vision and Acting on AIDS will have postcard campaigns on behalf of vulnerable children. These provide sound bites of information to send to your representative or senator in support of upcoming legislation. You can also make your own in support of upcoming votes on important legislation. They are easy to make and distribute, and they can be effective in educating leaders of the community and elected officials on important issues. Think of them as an easy, brief letter writing campaign to get the attention of your representative.

- *Write "Letters to the Editor."* Most magazines and newspapers include a "Letters to the Editor" page where readers can respond to a specific article, offering a critique or praise for the way the publication covered an issue. Follow the way your campus or community newspaper covers issues related to AIDS, and use these articles as an opportunity. Well thought out letters can be a counter argument for articles that do not support the ideals of caring for those affected by HIV and AIDS. They allow you to reach a larger audience and create an impression of widespread support for or against an issue.

Legislative Objectives

The following list contains specific legislative goals supported by World Vision and Acting on AIDS. These objectives focus on governmental actions that will benefit the biggest victims of the AIDS pandemic, primarily orphans and vulnerable children. This list can be used as a platform for your advocacy campaigns.

- The Global Fund to Fight AIDS, Tuberculosis, and Malaria (GFATM) was established in 2002 under the urging of the United Nations to dramatically increase the amount of funding available to fight AIDS, tuberculosis, and malaria. Funding is mainly provided by governments and foundations, such as the Bill & Melinda Gates Foundation. World Vision believes that the Global Fund is a valuable multilateral mechanism for funding AIDS programs globally. It calls on the U.S. government to fully fund its share of GFATM's needs (total needs are $7 billion). The United States contributed $100 million when the Global Fund was founded. When the President's Emergency Plan for AIDS Relief (PEPFAR) was launched in 2003, President George W. Bush proposed an additional $1 billion in support for the Global Fund over five years. By the end of 2007, the total U.S. contribution to the Global Fund will exceed $2 billion. The Global Fund is intended to complement bilateral and multilateral assistance programs, including PEPFAR. (PEPFAR is the largest international health initiative dedicated to a single disease in history. It is a 5-year, $15 billion global initiative to combat the HIV/AIDS epidemic by supporting treatment for 2 million people, prevention for 7 million, and care for 10 million.)

- World Vision urges the U.S. government leaders to continue to increase global AIDS funding each year with 10% dedicated to the care of orphans and vulnerable children as called for in the United States Leadership Against HIV and AIDS, Tuberculosis, and Malaria Act of 2003. This act was created to fund PEPFAR and works to see that 10% of these funds are earmarked for orphans and vulnerable children.

- World Vision asks the U.S. government to adopt policies and programs that prevent new infections primarily among children, mothers, and people at high risk of infection; we also ask for policies and programs to care for orphans and vulnerable children.

- Once the global AIDS legislation expires in 2008, World Vision will work to reauthorize this legislation. World Vision will continue to push for higher levels of funding, especially for orphans and vulnerable children.

Web Sites on Advocacy, Legislation, and Politics

These Web sites will provide you with additional information on the topics covered in this chapter. All of these are rich resources that will give you more background as you get involved in political advocacy.

- *Worldvision.org/actingonaids* offers guidelines for starting your own Acting on AIDS campus chapter.

- *Worldvision.org* highlights ways to get involved in global relief.

- *Networklobby.org* is a Web site for social justice, created by NETWORK, a national Catholic justice lobby. The legislative action center link on the site includes many helpful tools for lobbying Congress and local elected officials. It also details the steps to a bill becoming a law.

- *Seekjustice.org* is World Vision's Web site that provides the latest information on various issues of injustice around the world, such as HIV and AIDS, the use of children as soldiers in northern Uganda, and the sexual exploitation of children.

- *Thomas.loc.gov* supplies information on specific legislation; it is a service of the Library of Congress.

- *Vote-smart.org* is a non-partisan organization that tracks voting records and provides contact information of elected officials.

final thoughts

As people who have received the mercy of Jesus, it is the responsibility of Christians to extend his mercy to those in need. This includes the poor, the ill, victims of injustice, and those who are marginalized, including widows and orphans. The AIDS pandemic offers an opportunity for this generation to act on behalf of the destitute. As his representatives on earth, Christ calls his followers to respond to this crisis. The sad truth is that the church has responded slowly to the devastation. But the only way that the situation is hopeless is if you don't respond.

If you would like to be part of the answer of hope to this crisis, visit www.worldvision.org/actingonaids for more information on how to start your own chapter and transform your campus for the sake of those desperate for mercy. You can also contact Acting on AIDS directly at actingonaids@worldvision.org. There is also information at the back of this book for how to start your own Acting on AIDS chapter.

When Lily was 13 years old and still in school, a street peddler lured her into marrying him. Lily's parents, who are very poor, strongly opposed the marriage, but the couple decided to elope. Once married, Lily dropped out of school and lived with her husband in a slum on the outskirts of Mymensingh in Bangladesh. A year later, Lily became pregnant and had a baby girl. Soon after her daughter was born, her husband deserted her for another woman.

With nowhere to turn and no money, Lily returned to her family. Since she had not heeded her parents' advice, they rejected her. Lily's in-laws also turned her away. Now Lily and her daughter live at the railway platform in Mymensingh, under plastic sheeting hitched to a brick wall. With a poor education and no job skills, the sex trade was Lily's only resort for survival.

While conducting a survey among commercial sex workers, the staff of World Vision's Mymensingh HIV/AIDS Project met Lily and invited her to a seminar on HIV and AIDS. Through this program, Lily heard about the dangers of HIV for the first time. Lily continues her work for the sake of her child and her own survival, but now she is very cautious about the dangers.

The HIV/AIDS Project in Mymensingh is working to establish safer behavior and attitude changes among the high-risk people groups—sex workers, drug addicts, rickshaw pullers, and at-risk youth. The project is new and its funding is specifically used to build awareness and to provide education of HIV through workshops, seminars, and discussion.

discussion questions

Q The beginning of this chapter discusses the importance of sharing God's vision for the poor and sick, building a strong prayer life, and becoming a strong disciple of God. Do you think these things are related to the fight against AIDS? Do you think you currently have a strong foundation in these areas? Are you currently plugged in to a community that will help you grow in these areas? If not, what are some things you can do to address this?

Q This chapter touched on the importance of creativity in advocacy to communicate a message and make sure others feel the effects of AIDS. Do you agree that this is an important tool in advocacy? Talk about what makes the "Do You See Orange?" "Lives Are at Stake," and Anderson's bell-ringing campaign effective. Brainstorm some other campaign ideas, or even small elements of a campaign, that could communicate the impact of AIDS in a creative way.

Q What do you think of the idea that "advocacy is a privilege and responsibility"? How do you feel about the ability to use your American citizenship to try to affect positive change in the world? Is this something you've tried before? Why or why not? Discuss the pros and cons of working within the system of our representative government.

action items

1. Go through the list of Web sites listed in this chapter and spend time exploring each one. Find out the names of your local and state representatives, if you don't know them already, and whether they are involved in a committee related to AIDS or are active on this issue.

2. This chapter describes several ways to get involved in the fight against AIDS. Reread the section "Tools of Advocacy," decide which approach you'd like to take, and get started. Or, get together with other students and start a campus-wide campaign, similar to the "Do You See Orange?" or "Lives Are at Stake" events to increase awareness. Motivate others to help you write letters and make phone calls to your elected officials.

3. Once you've read through this guide, pass it on to someone else. Ask them to read it and then join you in the fight against AIDS.

Launching Your Own Acting on AIDS Chapter

HIV is one of the most devastating viruses the world has ever faced. In order to combat AIDS, we need a counter-virus of compassionate action to spread across our campuses, churches, and communities. These three quick steps will help you form an Acting on AIDS chapter on campus.

1. **Organize.** Organize a leadership team to plan and direct your chapter's activities on campus. Let us know you are getting started too. You can e-mail actingonaids@worldvision.org or call (253) 815-1000. If you register as an official chapter, we can send you helpful resources, include you in national activities and opportunities, and connect you with other chapters in your area and around the nation.

2. **Strategize.** Develop a strategy for how your chapter will create awareness on your campus. Begin by scheduling dates for key events and campaigns. Learn from what other chapters have done, and tailor it to your specific campus culture.

3. **Mobilize.** After you have successfully spread awareness across your campus, you will be ready to direct students to action. There are many ways to get involved, such as creating awareness in your surrounding churches and communities; becoming political advocates for widows and orphans; raising resources for communities in need; creating a discipleship study on caring for the poor and diseased; and learning how to integrate HIV and AIDS awareness with your education and future vocation. World Vision's commitment is to help orphaned and vulnerable children internationally, but you may also want to consider engaging with people in your local area who are affected by HIV.

Again, the best way to get started is by registering as an official chapter, so that we can share resources, keep you informed, and connect you with other students who are a part of the Acting on AIDS movement. Learn how to get involved and join this national movement by contacting Acting on AIDS at actingonaids@worldvision.org or (253) 815-1000.

Maps

pg 8 – © 2005 UNAIDS/WHO
pg 17 – © 2005 UNAIDS/WHO
pg 18 – © 2005 UNAIDS/WHO
pg 19 – © 2006 UNAIDS/WHO

Photographs

pg 1 – © Creative**Solutions**/World Vision
pg 3 – © Creative**Solutions**/World Vision
pg 23 – © 2005 Karie Hamilton/World Vision
pg 24 – © 2005 Karie Hamilton/World Vision
pg 29 – © 2004 Jon Warren/World Vision
pg 30 – © 2004 Reena Samuel/World Vision
pg 32 – © 2005 Jon Warren/World Vision
pg 35 – © 1995 Mikel Flamm/World Vision
pg 37 – © 2005 Caleb Mpamei/World Vision
pg 38 – © 2005 Jon Warren/World Vision
pg 46 – © 2004 Amio Ascension/World Vision
pg 48 – © 2002 James East/World Vision
pg 55 – © 2006 Nigel Marsh/World Vision
pg 57 – © 2005 Elimasia Mngumi/World Vision
pg 59 – © 2001 Todd Bartel/World Vision
pg 66 – © Creative**Solutions**/World Vision
pg 68 – © Creative**Solutions**/World Vision

World Vision is a Christian relief and development organization dedicated to helping children and their communities worldwide reach their full potential by tackling the causes of poverty.

Motivated by our faith in Jesus, we serve the poor as a demonstration of God's unconditional love for all people.

Contact us at:
www.worldvisionresources.com
wvresources@worldvision.org
ph: (800) 777-7752 or (909) 463-2998; Fax (909) 463-2999

Who we are

World Vision is a Christian relief and development organization dedicated to helping children and their communities worldwide reach their full potential by tackling the causes of poverty.

Who we serve

Motivated by our faith in Jesus, we serve the poor—regardless of a person's religion, race, ethnicity, or gender—as a demonstration of God's unconditional love for all people.

How we serve

Our passion is for the world's poorest children, whose suffering breaks the heart of God. To help secure a better future for each child, we focus on lasting, community-based transformation. We partner with individuals and communities, empowering them to develop sustainable access to clean water, food supplies, health care, education, and economic opportunities.

The ways we serve

In our work we bear witness to Jesus Christ in ways that encourage people to respond to the gospel. Since 1950,

- Emergency assistance to children and families affected by natural disasters and civil conflict.

- Developing long-term solutions within communities to alleviate poverty.

- Advocating for justice on behalf of the poor.

Putting our faith into action

Partnering with World Vision provides tangible ways to honor God and put faith into action, using the blessings He has given to serve the poor. By working together, all of us can make a real and lasting difference in the lives of children and families who are struggling to overcome poverty.

www.worldvision.org

endnotes

Introduction

[1] UNAIDS Questions and Answers (New York: UNAIDS, 2006).

[2] UNAIDS press release (New York: UNAIDS, 2001).

[3] *Global AIDS Report* (New York: UNAIDS, 2006).

[4] *Global AIDS,* 2006.

[5] U.S. Bureau of Census, report WP/98, World Population Profile: 1998, U.S. Government Printing Office, Washington DC, 1999, 62.

Chapter 1

[1] *AIDS Epidemic Update* (New York: UNAIDS, December 2005), 1–3.

[2] Norman Cantor, *In the Wake of the Plague: The Black Death and the World It Made* (New York: Perennial, 2002), 7.

[3] During WWII 52.2 million soldiers and civilians were killed. Source: World War II page, Historyplace.com (March 24, 2004) <www.historyplace.com/worldwar2/timeline/statistics.htm>.

[4] John M. Barry, *The Great Influenza: The Epic Story of the Deadliest Plague in History* (New York, NY: Penguin Group, 2004), 397.

[5] *Global AIDS Report* (New York: UNAIDS, 2004).

[6] *Children on the Brink: A Joint Report on Orphan Estimates and Program Strategies,* (New York: UNICEF, 2002), 30.

[7] *HIV and Infant Feeding: A UNICEF Fact Sheet* (New York: UNICEF, 2002), 2.

[8] Dale Hanson Bourke, *The Skeptic's Guide to the Global AIDS Crisis* (Tyrone, Ga.: Authentic, 2004), 9.

[9] Bourke, *Skeptic's Guide,* 14.

[10] UNAIDS, 2005, 3.

[11] Ibid., 3.

[12] Bourke, *Skeptic's Guide,* 5.

[13] Bourke, *Skeptic's Guide,* 5.

[14] Bourke, *Skeptic's Guide,* 14.

[15] UNAIDS, 2005, 17–30.

[16] *AIDS Epidemic,* 2005, 31.

[17] *AIDS Epidemic,* 2005, 33.

[18] *AIDS Epidemic,* 2005, 31–44.

[19] *AIDS Epidemic,* 2005, 5–52.

[20] *AIDS Epidemic,* 2005, 3.

[21] *AIDS Epidemic,* 2005, 53–64.

[22] *AIDS Epidemic,* 2005, 65–69.

[23] Ibid.

[24] Ibid.

[25] Ibid.

Chapter 2

[1] *Global AIDS Report* (New York: UNAIDS, 2004).

[2] Literacy and Non Formal Education Site, UNESCO Institute for Statistics (Sept. 2004) <www.unesco.org>.

[3] *Learning How to Survive: How Education for All Would Save Millions of Young People from HIV and AIDS* (London: Oxfam, 2004).

[4] Laurie Garrett. *HIV and National Security: Where are the Links?* (Council on Foreign Relations, New York, 2005).

[5] Women and HIV/AIDS: Confronting the Crisis, a joint report by UNAIDS, UNFPA, and UNIFEM, http://www.unfpa.org/hiv/women/report/chapter7.html.

[6] Anne Case, et. al, *Orphans in Africa* (Princeton: Princeton University Center for Health and Wellbeing, Research Program in Development Studies, 2003).

[7] Klaus Deininger, et. al, *AIDS-Induced Orphanhood as a Systemic Shock: Magnitude, Impact and Program Interventions in Africa* (Washington, D.C.: World Bank, 2003).

[8] C. Coombe, "Mitigating the Impact of HIV and AIDS on Education Supply, Demand, and Quality," *AIDS, Policy, and Child Well-Being*, ed. by A. Cornia. (New York: UNICEF, 2002).

[9] Mbulawa Mugabe, et. al, *Future Imperfect: Protecting Children on the Brink* (Johannesburg: Africa Leadership Consultation, 2002).

[10] James Sengendo and Janet Nambi, "The Psychological Effect of Orphanhood: A Study of Orphans in the Rakai District." *Health Transition Review*, 7 (sup.), (1997): 105–124.

[11] Minki Chatterji, et. al, *The Well-Being of Children Affected by HIV and AIDS in Lusaka, Zambia, and Gitarama Province, Rwanda: Findings from a Study* (Washington, D.C.: USAID, 2005).

[12] Peter Singer, "Caution: Children at War," *Parameters* (Winter 2001): 40–56.

[13] Masimba Tafirenyika, "Restoring Lost Childhood in Sierra Leone: UN and NGOs Run Programmes to Reintegrate Former Child Soldiers," *Africa Recovery*, 15, no. 3 (October 2001): 12.

[14] UN Chronicle, "Ten Stories the World Should Hear More About," Volume XLI, Number 2, 2004.

[15] HIV/AIDS and Food Scarcity, UN Food and Agriculture Organization (February 1, 2005) <www.fao.org/hivaids/>.

[16] Rachel Waterhouse, *The Impact of HIV/AIDS on Farmers' Knowledge of Seed: Case Study of Chokwe District, Gaza Province, Mozambique*, (International Crops Research Institute for the Semi-Arid Tropics, 2004).

[17] R. Loewenson and A. Whiteside, *HIV/AIDS: Implications for Poverty Reduction* (New York: UNDP Policy Paper, 2001).

[18] Sharon LaFraniere, "AIDS and Custom Leave African Families Nothing," *New York Times* (February 18, 2005).

[19] *Widening the 'Window of Hope': Using Food Aid to Improve Access to Education for Orphans and Vulnerable Children in sub-Saharan Africa* (World Food Programme, 2003), 4.

[20] World Health Organization, "Malaria and HIV Interactions and Their Implications for Public Health Policy" Report of a Technical Consultation (Geneva, Switzerland, June 23–25, 2004), 9.

[21] Ibid., 9.

[22] African Communities against Malaria (June 9, 2006) <www.acamalaria.org>.

[23] WHO, "Malaria," 1.

[24] Oxfam, 2004, 4.

[25] *Basic Statistic in Education: 1995–1999* (Dar es Salaam, United Republic of Tanzania, Ministry of Education and Culture, 2000).

[26] Education Statistics Page, Ministry of Education and Sports, Government of Uganda (March 22, 2006) <http://www.education.go.ug/abstract_2004.htm>.

[27] Luis Crouch, *Turbulence or Orderly Change? Teacher Supply and Demand in the Age of AIDS* (Pretoria: Department of Education South Africa, 2001).

[28] Ibid., 2001.

[29] *Future Forsaken: Abuses Against Children Affected by HIV/AIDS in India.* (New York: Human Rights Watch, 2004)

[30] Laura Nyblad, et. al, *Disentangling HIV and AIDS Stigma in Ethiopia, Tanzania, and Zambia* (International Center for Research on Women, 2003).

[31] Lee-Nah Hsu, *HIV Subverts National Security*, (United Nations Development Programme, 2001), 4.

[32] Mark Schneider and Michael Moodie, *The Destabilizing Impacts of HIV/AIDS.* (Washington, D.C.: Center for Strategic and International Studies, 2002), 7.

[33] Ibid., 6.

[34] Peter Singer, "AIDS and International Security," *Survival* 44 (spring 2002): 145–158.

[35] Barks-Ruggles, et. al, *The Economic Impact of HIV and AIDS in Southern Africa.* (Brookings Institution, Conference Report, no. 9, September 2001): 4.

[36] Sydney Rosen and Jonathan L. Simon, *Shifting the Burden of HIV and AIDS.* (Center for International Health, Boston University School of Public Health, February 2002), 2.

[37] *HIV/AIDS As a Security Issue.* (Washington, D.C./Brussels: UNAIDS/International Crisis Group Report, 2001), 2.

[38] Clive Bell, et. al, *The Long-Run Economic Costs of AIDS: Theory and an Application to South Africa* (Washington, D.C.: World Bank, 2003), 45.

[39] Ibid.

Chapter 3

[1] Christian Connections for International Health, "Does the ABC Approach Demand an Unrealistic Standard of Behavior?" *The ABC Approach to Preventing the Sexual Transmission of HIV: Common Questions and Answers* (May 2006), 29.

[2] Dr. Edward C. Green, *Rethinking AIDS Prevention: Learning from Successes in Developing Countries*, (London: Praeger, 2003), 141–262.

[3] Ibid., 151–152.

[4] Ibid., 143.

[5] A decline in prevalence must be preceded by a decline in infections. The 7- to 10-year-cycle from HIV infection to mortality causes the HIV-prevalence rate—the number of people living with HIV as a percentage of the total population—to rise or fall with a lag to changes in the rate of new HIV infections. Given the long HIV infection period, HIV incidence had to decrease sharply before 1991 to produce a peak and a drop in prevalence. Source: Green, *Rethinking*, 141–262.

[6] R. Turner, "Young Ugandans Know Condoms Prevent STDs, But Disagree on Whether Use Shows Respect for Partner," *International Family Planning Perspectives* 19, no.2 (June 1993): 76.

[7] Green, *Rethinking*, 157.

[8] Turner, "Young Ugandans," 76.

[9] D. Brown, "Uganda's AIDS Decline Attributable to Deaths," *Washington Post*, 24, (February 2005), <www.washingtonpost.com/wp-dyn/articles/A48464-2005Feb23.

html?sub%253Dnew>.

[10] Green, *Rethinking*, 103–104.

[11] *Report on the Global AIDS Epidemic*, (New York: UNAIDS, 2006): 506.

[12] Green, *Rethinking*, 143.

[13] Timothy C. Morgan, "Why We're Losing the War Against AIDS," *Christianity Today*, 7 (March 2005).

[14] Christian Connections for International Health, "Are Condoms Effective Against HIV/ AIDS?" *The ABC Approach to Preventing the Sexual Transmission of HIV: Common Questions and Answers* (May 2006): 17–20, 51.

[15] Krambeer, et. al, "Methadone Therapy for Opioid Dependence," *American Family Physician* (June 2001) <www.aafp.org/afp/20010615/2404.html>.

[16] Avins, et. al, "Changes in HIV-Related Behaviors among Heterosexual Alcoholics Following Addiction Treatment," *Drug and Alcohol Dependence* 44, no. 1 (1997): 47–55.

[17] Guydish, et. al, "Evaluating Needle Exchange: Are There Negative Effects?" *AIDS* 7, no. 6 (June 1993): 871–876.

[18] Marx, et. al, "Impact of Needle Exchange Programs on Adolescent Perceptions about Illicit Drug Use," *AIDS and Behavior* 5, no. 4 (December 2001): 379–386.

[19] Schechter, et. al, "Do Needle Exchange Programmes Increase the Spread of HIV among Injection Drug Users? An Investigation of the Vancouver Outbreak," *AIDS* 13, no. 6 (April 1999): F45–F51.

[20] Hagan, et. al, "Sharing of Drug Preparation Equipment as a Risk Factor for Hepatitis C," *American Journal of Public Health* 91, no. 1 (2001): 42–46.

[21] "Microfinance in China: Growth and Struggle," *Special Section: How Some Industries Are Responding to Growth Opportunities in China,* Knowledge @ Wharton (May 2006), <www.knowledge.wharton.upenn.edu/article/1471.cfm>.

[22] Jill Donahue, *Forward Looking Review: World Vision's Approaches to Integrating Microenterprise Development and HIV/AIDS Response,* (Johannesburg: World Vision, 2005).

[23] *Integrating Microfinance with HIV/AIDS Care* (Federal Way, Wa.: World Vision, 2006), 2.

[24] The World Bank (April 18, 2005), <web.worldbank.org/WBSTIE/EXTERNAL/TOPICS/ EXTEDUCATION/O,,contentMDK;20591648~menuPK:282393~pagePK:148956~piPK:21 6618~theSitePK:282386,00.html>.

[25] *Learning to Survive: How Education for All Would Save Millions of Young People from HIV/AIDS* (London: Oxfam, 2004).

[26] Education for All Site, The World Bank (May 30, 2006), <web.worldbank.org/WBSTIE/ EXTERNAL/TOPICS/EXTEDUCATION0,,contentMDK:20374062~menuPK:540090~pag ePK:148956~piPK:216618~theSitePK:282386,00.html>.

[27] Millennium Development Goals Site, United Nations (May 31, 2006), <www.un.org/ millenniumgoals>.

[28] Multilateral Debt Relief Initiative Fact Site, International Monetary Fund (May 31, 2006), <www.imf.org/external/np/exr/facts/mdri.htm>. The G-8 countries are Canada, France, Germany, Italy, Japan, Russia, the U.K., and the U.S.

[29] Heavily Indebted Poor Countries fact site, International Monetary Fund (May 31, 2006), <www.imf.org/external/x10/changecss/changestyle.aspx>.

[30] MDRI Site, International Monetary Fund, 2006.

[31] *100% Debt Relief for HIPC Countries from International Financial Institutions* (Washington, D.C.: DATA, June 2004) <www.data.org/policy/debt/pdf/100_DATA_Jun04.pdf>.

[32] UNAIDS, 2004, 506.

[33] It is estimated that there are two vulnerable children for every child orphaned by AIDS. Source:

Ruxin, et. al, *Combating AIDS in the Developing World: Achieving the Millennium Development Goals* (London: Earthscan, 2005).

34 In its 2004 *Children on the Brink* report, UNICEF said that there will be 18.4 million children orphaned by AIDS and a total of 50 million children orphaned by all causes, in sub-Saharan Africa by 2010. Using the convention of two vulnerable children for every child orphaned by AIDS, we arrive at a total of 50 million orphans and 36.8 million vulnerable children, or 86.8 million orphans and vulnerable children (OVC). UNICEF also estimates that there will be 400 million total children in sub-Saharan Africa in 2010. This means that 22%, or more than 1 out of every 5 children in sub-Saharan Africa will be either orphaned due to AIDS and all other causes or vulnerable due to AIDS by 2010.

35 Marins, et. al, "Dramatic Improvement in Survival among Adult Brazilian AIDS Patients," *AIDS* 17 (2003): 1675–1682.; Kathy Attawell and Jackie Mundy, *Provision of Antiretroviral Therapy in Resource Limited Settings: A Review of Experience up to August 2003* (London: DFID/WHO, 2003); Pascual Ortells, *Brazil: A Model Response to AIDS* (Interhemispheric Resource Center, Americas Program, 2003); M. Vitoria, *Monitoring System for the Antiretroviral Therapy in Brazil: Lessons Learned and Future Direction* (WHO/UNAIDS, Workshop on Strategic Information for Anti-Retroviral Therapy Programmes, 2003).

36 Ortells, *Brazil*, 2003; Attawell and Mundy, *Provision*, 2003.

37 Attawell and Mundy, *Provision*, 2003.

38 Attawell and Mundy, *Provision*, 2003.

39 *Care for Children Affected by HIV/AIDS: The Urgent Need for International Standards* (New York/Geneva: UNICEF/International Social Service, 2004), 4.

40 UNICEF's five key elements of an effective program of care and support for OVC are: (1) Strengthen the capacity of families to protect and care for orphans and vulnerable children by prolonging the lives of parents and providing economic, psychosocial and other support. (2) Mobilize and support community-based responses. (3) Ensure access for orphans and vulnerable children to essential services, including education, health care, birth registration and others. (4) Ensure that governments protect the most vulnerable children through improved policy and legislation and by channeling resources to families and communities. (5) Raise awareness at all levels through advocacy and social mobilization to create a supportive environment for children and families affected by HIV and AIDS. Source: UNAIDS, *The Framework for the Protection, Care, and Support of Orphans and Vulnerable Children Living in a World with HIV and AIDS* (New York: UNICEF, 2004).

41 Laura Deame, *A Generation of Orphans: Another Challenge for AIDS-Ravaged Countries* (World Resources Institute, Earth Trends, 2001) (May 31, 2006), <earthtrends.wri.org/features/view_feature.php?theme=4&fid=22>.

42 Average of World Vision costing exercises in Kenya and Uganda (winter 2005) and Zambia and Mozambique (spring 2005), available on the World Vision HIV/AIDS Library website <www.worldvision.org/help/aids-lib.nsf>.

Chapter 4

1 Liz Carty, et. al., *Just Add Consciousness: A Guide to Social Activism* (Washington, D.C.: Oxfam America, 2000), 2.

2 Ibid, 5.

362.1969
H1777

A Guide to Acting on AIDS *tells how one of the biggest issues fac-ing the world today is HIV and AIDS. And I believe that the Church holds the answer. It is essential that the next generation understands and acts upon this crisis and the injustices behind it, as we point to the saving hope of Jesus Christ.*

—TOBYMAC

A Guide to Acting on AIDS *shows how people of all ages can respond to the global AIDS crisis. Through organizations like World Vision that are operational in every sense, we have an arm of the church that is equipped to serve those in need—if everyone lends their voice and resources to help.*

—TONY HALL
Retired U.S. Congressman, and Ambassador to the United Nations

I cannot think of anything more significant in the battle against the global AIDS pandemic than getting this next generation of young adults all around the world fully educated, empowered, and engaged through local churches as active agents of change.

—KAY WARREN
Executive Director – HIV/AIDS Initiative, Saddleback Church

My friends at Acting on AIDS have done a terrific service in preparing this book. In one read, we can learn about the disease, learn who is being affected, and be guided in our attempts to contribute toward a solution. Will you read this book in its entirety? Will you pass this book along to somebody else? Will you become a part of the solution?

—DONALD MILLER
Author of *Blue Like Jazz*